Overcoming Overload

OVERCOMING OVERLOAD

STEVE & MARY FARRAR

Multnomah®Publishers *Sisters, Oregon*

OVERCOMING OVERLOAD
published by Multnomah Publishers, Inc.

© 2003 by Steve and Mary Farrar

Published in association with the literary agency of Alive Communications, Inc.,
7610 Goddard Street, Suite 200, Colorado Springs, Colorado, 80920.

International Standard Book Number: 1-59052-084-X

Cover image by Getty Images/Dave Nagel

Unless otherwise indicated, Scripture quotations are from:
New American Standard Bible® © 1960, 1977, 1995
by the Lockman Foundation. Used by permission.

Other Scripture quotations are from:
The Holy Bible, New International Version (NIV) © 1973, 1984 by International
Bible Society, used by permission of Zondervan Publishing House

The Message by Eugene H. Peterson © 1993, 1994, 1995, 1996, 2000
Used by permission of NavPress Publishing Group All rights reserved.

The Holy Bible, New King James Version (NKJV) © 1984 by Thomas Nelson, Inc.
Italics in Scripture quotations are author's emphasis.

Multnomah is a trademark of Multnomah Publishers, Inc.,
and is registered in the U.S. Patent and Trademark Office.
The colophon is a trademark of Multnomah Publishers, Inc.

Printed in the United States of America

Library of Congress Cataloging-in-Publication Data
Farrar, Steve.
    Overcoming overload / by Steve and Mary Farrar.
        p. cm.
Includes bibliographical references (p. 241)
    ISBN 1-59052-084-X
    1. Christian life. 2. Stress (Psychology)--Religious aspects--Christianity. I. Farrar,
Mary. II. Title.
    BV4509.5.F35 2003
    248.8'6--dc21   2002155910

03 04 05 06 07 08—10 9 8 7 6 5 4 3 2 1 0

To Rachel,
our precious lamb—may you always find rest
and refreshment in His pasture.

CONTENTS

Acknowledgments 9

1. Tired of Being Tired 11

2. The Pause That Refreshes: *You Need a Sabbath* 33

3. Solitary Refinement: *You Need a Sanctuary* 65

4. Real Food in a Fast Food Nation:
   You Need Sustenance 91

5. Decompression Chamber: *You Need Supplication* . . 119

6. Affluenza: *You Need to Simplify* 151

7. Two Feet of Bark: *You Need a Sovereign* 177

8. Two Slabs of Timber: *You Need a Savior* 207

Epilogue: *Dying to Live* 237

Notes 241

ACKNOWLEDGMENTS

Mary and I have never written a book together before. Both of us have written books separately, but up until now, we had never attempted one as a joint venture.

The question was, "How do we do this without killing each other?" Well, the book is finished, and we are both alive and still friends. We can't quite explain how that took place other than to credit the grace of God.

There is something that must be clarified up front. Together we have worked on every page and paragraph. But in order to keep confusion at a minimum, you can assume that the text is coming through Steve's voice. After a while, our two voices got so mingled it became difficult for us to make a distinction between the two. But we think that's a good thing.

When we began this process, we had a wonderful schedule all sketched out that would enable us to write the book without getting overloaded. And then Mary got sick with a virus and was in bed for close to six weeks. Needless to say, we suddenly both got overloaded. But Mary recovered and the great team at Multnomah was able to squeeze out a few extra weeks at the finish line for us.

Our good friend Larry Libby, along with Michael Christopher, sharpened the text, put the dots over the i's, and crossed the t's in their unique fashion. A special thank you goes to Doug Gabbert for juggling nine or ten balls in the production process, which gave us the extra space we needed.

Chuck Swindoll and David Chavanne were kind enough to allow Steve to teach this material from scratch to the congregation at Stonebriar Community Church in Frisco, Texas. And Nancy Lyons kept the office together with her special touch during the entire process.

To these and many more we are grateful.

—*Steve and Mary Farrar*

Chapter One

TIRED OF BEING TIRED

"The house of my soul is too small for You to come to it.
May it be enlarged by You.
It is in ruins; restore it."

AUGUSTINE

I f there is one term that describes the state of affairs in the lives of people today, it is *overload.* The mere mention of the word triggers an audible groan or sigh within us. *Overload* reminds us of the weight of everyday life. We are overwhelmed, overworked, overcommitted, overanxious, overmatched and overextended. Our tanks are on empty and we're running on fumes.

Have you ever been in a health club and seen someone sprinting on a treadmill? That's the mental picture that comes to mind. We're running as fast as we can to keep from falling off the back, and we desperately need to stop that relentless machine and take a breather. But we can't seem to find a button that will turn the thing off.

So we keep running. For weeks. Months. Maybe years. And we are running with a huge pack on our backs, full of all the important things in our lives. Things like family, career, athletics, financial plans, personal goals, and "to do" lists. The trouble is, all of that running is beginning to catch up with us. We're overloaded from the weight and overloaded from the race.

We're worn out. Exhausted. What has brought us to such a state? Even the wisest, healthiest, and most capable among us feel it. There is a collective sense among us that our personal worlds are spinning out of control, and as the pace of life increases exponentially, we despair of ever gaining the upper hand.

Overload is really just another way to say *overwhelmed.*

Does that strike a chord with you?

The thing is, not everyone is overwhelmed for the same reason.

Some of us are overwhelmed by the *pace* of life. Some of us are overwhelmed by the *pressures* of life. Some of us are overwhelmed by the *pain* of life.

As you diagnose your own set of circumstances, which one of the three best fits you? Perhaps it's a combination of more than one. The pace, pressures, and pain of life each demand a closer look.

OVERWHELMED BY THE PACE OF LIFE

Have you heard the term *24/7?*

Of course you have. It popped into our language within the last few years, and now it's everywhere. I don't remember my parents using the term when I was growing up in the '50s. I don't remember it from my high school years in the '60s or my college days in the early '70s. I don't even recall hearing it in the '80s. But sometime in the last ten years or so, it has become a mantra of our American culture. *Twenty-four* refers to twenty-four hours and *7* stands for the seven days of the week. 24/7 has become the standard American pace. It's twenty-four hours a day, seven days a week.

In other words, nonstop.

But that's only part of the story. We not only live in a world of 24/7, we live in a world of *more*. In his thought-provoking book, *Hurtling Toward Oblivion*, Richard Swenson describes the condition well:

> No matter where we look—it makes no difference—there is always more. No matter what topic we consider—there is always more.
>
> Obviously there are more people—lots of people.
>
> There are more cars traveling more miles over more roads, and more airplanes carrying more passengers on more flights.… There are more computers, more books, and more magazines, all processing

and distributing more information—lots more information.

There are more businesses offering more services and making more products—lots more products. There are more buildings, more restaurants, more medications, more telephones, and more money. Lots more money.

There are more activities and commitments, more choices and decisions, more change and stress, more technology and complexity.

There is, in short, more…of everything. Wherever we look, we are surrounded by more. Always."[1]

Thirty years ago, a very insightful man made this observation: "Everything grows: Everything is on the increase, *and every year the speed of that increase is greater*."[2] Robert Vacca made that observation in 1969. Has the speed of life picked up since then? It has increased exponentially. And it continues to accelerate. If you have any doubt, consider the following facts:

- In 1800 there were *one* billion people; in 1930, *two* billion; 1960, *three* billion; 1975, *four* billion; 1987, *five* billion; and 1998, *six* billion.
- Life expectancy worldwide was twenty-one years at the time of Christ, forty-eight years in 1955, and

sixty-five years in 1995. This is expected to rise to eighty-five years by 2050.

- There are sixty-two thousand new book titles and new editions each year.
- The *Physicians' Desk Reference (PDR)* had three hundred pages when it first came out 1948; fifty years later it has three thousand pages.
- In 1978, the average grocery store had eleven thousand products; now it has over thirty thousand products.
- There are 550 different kinds of coffee, 250 different kinds of toothpaste, and 175 different kinds of salad dressing.
- There are 2,500 different types of lightbulbs—in one store alone.[3]

Will these trends slow down or stop anytime in the near future? Of course not. *More* just keeps on coming. If it slowed down, we would think something was wrong. Consider one more comment from Swenson:

The phenomenon of *more* I call profusion…wherever progress is most active, profusion is most active… progress always give us more and more of everything faster and faster.[4]

"Faster and faster." That pretty much describes the pace

of most of our lives, doesn't it? So back to the question. Why are we living at a pace that we know is too fast? I think it comes down to the fact that we have believed a lie—actually three lies.

Lie Number One: "You can have it all."

No you can't! You really can't. And even if you could, where would you put it? What would you do with it? Having it all would demand tremendous amounts of time and energy. Would it be worth the price?

It's a moot point, of course, because you *can't* have it all. If you still think you'd like to try to have it all, you could save yourself a lot of time by simply reading the Book of Ecclesiastes. A king by the name of Solomon authored that potent little book of the Bible, and he was a man who literally had it all.

Now, if it's a lie that you can have it all, how did Solomon manage to get it all? The answer is that Solomon is the one man who desired to have it all and who got it all because God wanted him to experience firsthand what that would be like, then record his observations for future generations—who would want it all, too.

Solomon spent his life accumulating everything he could possibly get his hands on (you can read a personal account of his quest in the first two chapters of Ecclesiastes). He had homes that would have made it into

Architectural Digest. He owned breathtaking vineyards and beautiful wineries. He maintained greenhouses full of exotic flowers and gorgeous gardens beyond imagination. He kept stable upon stable of Thoroughbred horses. He had wives, quite a few wives—seven hundred to be precise—along with three hundred concubines (just in case seven hundred wives weren't quite enough). Solomon never drank out of a Dixie Cup in his life. He only drank out of goblets made of gold (see 1 Kings 10:21). He described his effort to have it all in these words: *"All that my eyes desired I did not refuse them"* (Ecclesiastes 2:10).

Solomon outdid any other king on the face of the earth in his riches and possessions (see 1 Kings 10:23). And on top of all that, he was the wisest man who ever lived. When Solomon was a young man ascending the throne of his father, David, God offered to give him anything he requested. Solomon didn't ask for riches; he asked for wisdom. And because he asked for wisdom, God threw in the wealth and prosperity as a signing bonus. He was such a legend that the queen of Sheba visited him to see if what she'd heard about him was true. If there is any doubt that Solomon had it all, the queen of Sheba can take the stand as a material witness.

When the queen of Sheba perceived all the wisdom of Solomon, the house he had built, the food of his table, the seating of his servants, the attendance of his waiters and their attire, his cupbearers, and his stairway by which he went up to the house of the LORD, there was no more spirit in her.

Then she said to the king, "It was a true report which I heard in my own land about your words and your wisdom. Nevertheless I did not believe the reports, until I came and my eyes had seen it. And behold, the half was not told me. You exceed in wisdom and prosperity the report which I heard." (1 Kings 10:4–7)

King Solomon really did have it all. He managed to pull it off. It must have taken a tremendous amount of time and energy. (Just remembering birthdays and anniversaries for seven hundred wives would have been a little taxing.) He may have been the original guy to come up with *24/7*. He believed the lie, pursued the lie, and accomplished the lie.

And when he got there, he realized he had been deceived.

Having it all simply wasn't worth the effort. He was left with a handful of ashes. Here is his report on what it was like to have it all:

All that my eyes desired I did not refuse them. I did not withhold my heart from any pleasure, for my heart was pleased because of all my labor and this was my reward for all my labor....

So I hated life, for the work which had been done under the sun was grievous to me; because everything is futility and striving after wind.

Thus I hated all the fruit of my labor for which I had labored under the sun, for I must leave it to the man who will come after me. And who knows whether he will be a wise man or a fool? Yet he will have control over all the fruit of my labor for which I have labored by acting wisely under the sun. This too is vanity. Therefore I completely despaired of all the fruit of my labor for which I had labored under the sun. (Ecclesiastes 2:10, 17–20)

So much for the desire to have it all. Solomon was deeply disappointed. So why are you and I running faster and faster? After reading his assessment, I'm ready to take a couple of days off.

Lie Number Two: "You can do it all."

We know instinctively that there's no way we can do it all. But a quick review of our daily schedules might make an outside observer think otherwise. This lie shows itself in the number of commitments we sign off on. First of all, we overcommit our children.

It is not uncommon for one child to have the following commitments. School (at least eight hours, five days a week), homework (an average of two to three hours per night), piano lessons plus daily practice time, karate lessons, soccer team (one game per week plus five practices). That would be an average schedule for an average American child. And many children have additional commitments beyond these. Notice that the schedule doesn't allow any time for church and youth group activities.

A child with that kind of schedule has absolutely no downtime. There's no time to play. (Kids don't play anymore. They're placed on organized teams with thirty-something coaches who never made it athletically— coaches driven to make sure these eight-year-olds win the league championship or break their little hearts trying). Kids don't have time to read. They don't have time to read biographies of great leaders. They don't have time to draw or build stuff with LEGOs. They don't have time to be creative. They don't have time to enjoy their family and work through issues of conflict. The average American child is overwhelmed by the schedule that has been set for him.

Remember also that the above schedule is for one child only. When you multiply that schedule by three kids, life starts reeling out of control. Just take athletics, for example. Three kids equal three games per week plus fifteen practices per week. Plus they are in karate at least once a week. So that's three more weekly lessons.

With this kind of schedule, when is there any time to have dinner together at home? When is there any time to play catch? When is there any time to take a walk together around the neighborhood? With everything else going on, there is no time left for those kinds of activities.

We are living at a "Fibonacci" pace. A what? I was recently introduced to the concept of Fibonacci numbers. Unless you have an advanced degree in mathematics, you're probably unfamiliar with Fibonacci numbers. I certainly was. "Fibonacci" was the nickname of their discoverer, the fourteenth-century mathematician named Leonardo Pisano. Fibonacci numbers sound complex, but the underlying concept is actually quite simple.

"Fibonacci numbers consist of adding together the two previous numbers to create the current one: 1, 1, 2, 3, 5, 8, 13, 21, 34, 55, 89, 144."[5]

As soon as the concept of a Fibonacci number was explained to me, I thought to myself, That's *how we get so busy in life!* It's easy to get overloaded very quickly when you're playing with Fibonacci numbers.

Let's say your life is already loaded with six major responsibilities. And then along come two other issues that you have to carry and handle. According to normal math, that means your six current responsibilities plus two more equal eight. But on the Fibonacci scale you are suddenly at a much, much higher number! The eighth number in the Fibonacci sequence is not eight; it is twenty-one! Every new stress or responsibility brings more to the equation than what you'd have if you added just one thing.

You can get "Fibonaccied" even if your children are grown and out on their own. It's possible at any place in life to get overcommitted and overloaded. A friend was recently commenting about his retired parents. "They're exhausted," he said. "I thought retirement was supposed to be a time of slowing down and enjoying life. My folks are as stressed out as they've ever been. They can't seem to say no to anything."

No matter where we are in life, we are susceptible to giving in to the lie of "doing it all."

Lie Number Three: "You deserve it all."

This is another lie that contributes to a pace of life that is all out of balance. If you deserve it all, you are going to work 24/7 to make sure you get it. And you will run over anyone that gets in your way. I heard a story about an attorney that makes the point.

A local charity had never received a donation from the town's most successful lawyer. The director called to get a contribution.

"Our records show that you make $500,000 a year, yet you haven't given a penny to charity," the director began.

"Wouldn't you like to help the community?"

The lawyer replied, "Did your research show that my mother is ill, with medical bills several times her annual income?"

"Um, no," mumbled the director.

"Or that my brother is blind and unemployed?" The stricken director began to stammer out an apology.

"Or that my sister's husband died in an accident," said the lawyer, his voice rising in indignation, "leaving her penniless and with three kids?"

The humiliated director said, "I had no idea."

"So," said the lawyer, "if I don't give any money to them, why would I give any to you?"

When someone begins to believe that they can have it all, can do it all, and deserve it all, someone else is going to get hurt. We've been reading too many true-life stories of top executives who drove their companies into bankruptcy while stockpiling millions away for themselves. They showed utter disregard for the shareholders and employees who were completely wiped out.

For years I have observed a number of men who have bought into those three big lies and left their wives and abandoned their children. Over the last few years, I have seen the same epidemic spread to more and more women as well. I have seen fine, Christian men and women become cold and callous toward their families. How did that happen? Somewhere along the line they began to believe they deserved it all.

I'm thinking of a Christian woman who recently went against the counsel of her church and divorced her husband. If five years ago you would have told her that she would do such a thing, she would have said you were crazy, and that she would *never* do such a thing. And five years ago she never would have considered divorce to be an option. Sure, she and her husband had some significant issues, but once upon a time, divorce was something that would never have been considered.

So what happened?

This was a family that lived at a breakneck pace. There was very little time for each other. There was very little time to nurture their relationship with the Lord by reading the Scriptures. It was go-go-go from early in the morning until late at night. And when our lives get so busy that we have no time for God and His truth, we become vulnerable to believing the lie.

The wrong pace can lead to wrong decisions.

Pace is not just a scheduling issue. For the Christian, it is a *life* issue.

OVERWHELMED BY THE PRESSURES OF LIFE

If the pace of life doesn't overwhelm you, then the pressure will. I saw a cartoon the other day that made me laugh out loud. Two raccoons were on a deserted highway in the middle of the night reading a billboard advertisement for an insomnia clinic. The faces of the raccoons registered deep concern as they read the two questions on the billboard:

Do you have dark circles under your eyes?
Do you stay awake at night?

The raccoons had nothing to worry about—except, perhaps, about people who drive as fast as they live. But we do. Why do so many of us have dark circles under our eyes and find that we cannot sleep? It's the pressures of life. For many of us, there is just no more breathing room in our lives. Our lives are full to the brim. Yet every day brings more commitments and more pressures that demand to be squeezed in.

Pressure can come to us in two ways.

It can come, first, from our own conscious choices in life.

God designed us as human beings to carry a certain amount of pressure. But we are finite. "We are but dust," says the psalmist (Psalm 103:14). And too much pressure will inevitably bring us down. Too much pressure makes our heads ache, brings pain to our chests, and sets our nerves on edge. We simply are not equipped for too much pressure.

Epicureanism says, "Be sensuous; enjoy yourself." Education says, "Be resourceful; expand yourself." Materialism says, "Be satisfied; please yourself." Psychology says, "Be confident; fulfill yourself." Pride says, "Be superior; promote yourself." Humanism says, "Be capable; believe in yourself." But God says to us, "Be wise; humble yourself."

The world drives us to achieve and acquire more. But God cautions us to stop and listen to Him. He has told us clearly in Scripture how to live life, and when we depart from His plan, as our culture has, many lives and many families collapse.

But pressure can also come from circumstances over which we have no control…the painful, unexpected things that overwhelm and overload us.

OVERWHELMED BY THE PAIN OF LIFE

Things happen to us that deeply wound us, that cut us to the very core of our being. I recently talked with a man that I respect very much. He is a mature Christian and highly respected in his community. He told me about one of his adult children, a son who made a very poor ethical decision that affected not only himself, but also a number of other people. His decision had life-shattering consequences.

As the grieving father related this tragic event, he literally began to double over in his chair. Ever so slightly, he leaned forward like someone experiencing stomach cramps. He didn't realize he was doing it, but as he was talking, he folded himself up on the edge of his chair. The pain of what he was describing went so deep that he began to knot up inside. It wouldn't have been much worse if someone had kicked him in the stomach.

You've probably felt that way a few times in your life. Maybe you've been betrayed by someone you trusted or loved. The devastation was so awful it took your breath away. It might have been your best friend, your spouse, your child, or your business partner. And when you got the news—when it really dawned on you what had happened—it cut you as deep as you've ever been cut in your life.

Oh, man, that's pain.

A son you have raised to know the Lord makes some life decisions that are so contrary to how he's been raised that you can't sleep at night. A daughter who was once the joy and sunshine of your life has turned cold, hard, and unresponsive. There are no pills you can swallow that assuage that kind of pain. It's just too deep, slicing into the very fiber of who you are. You see, it isn't always the pace of life that throws us into overload; sometimes it's just sheer, bone-deep pain.

It could be the loss of your retirement savings in the stock market downturn or the news that you have cancer. Whatever the source of the pain, it slaps us off our feet and washes over us like an ocean wave. And we find ourselves disoriented and gasping for breath.

When our lives get overloaded from the pace of life or the pressures of life or the pain of life, we're going to get overwhelmed.

DEFICIT LIVING

Overload is a symptom of deficit living. Overloaded people live in deficit—emotional, relational, or spiritual. When our checking accounts are overdrawn, we experience immediate stress and pressure, don't we? It sets off an adrenal rush to find a way to immediately cover that shortfall. But where do you find a surplus when you're already short? Where do you get money when you're completely out?

It's also possible to get overdrawn in life. When we are overwhelmed we find ourselves living in deficit—emotional deficit, relational deficit, spiritual deficit. We get overdrawn in our marriages and overdrawn with our kids. We run out of currency—the emotional and relational "cash" that it takes to live life well. And before long we begin to get anxious and panicky, because we think there is no way out.

J. I. Packer describes this bleak, hopeless condition:

> If we come to think or feel (often we are not quite rational about this) that we have nothing to hope for and can only expect things to get worse in the future, inevitably we grow depressed and, to a degree, desperate. We may try to hide our condition, but the unfocused rage, fury and hatred of life that we feel work like acid, dissolving all other feelings into purest bitterness. Hopelessness is at the root of many of today's

psychological disorders…. And even when hopeless-
ness is only fitful and intermittent, a mood that pos-
sesses until it passes, it still makes us feel alone, afraid
and paralyzed for action.

We find that we cannot make decisions nor bring
ourselves to do things. Our sense of self-worth dis-
solves into self-doubt, self-distrust, and self-dislike;
confidence is swallowed up in despair. We find ourselves in a tunnel that has no light at the end of it,
only deeper darkness and eventually a blank wall."[6]

Long-term overload can rob us of hope. And hope is the
oxygen of the soul. As Thomas Fuller observed, "If it were
not for hopes, the heart would break."

So are you overloaded? Has it been a long-term condition?

THE ATM OF HOPE

To be overloaded is to be without the spiritual cash that it
takes to live life well. God has provided for each of us an
unlimited line of credit in His Word. The Bible is not
unlike an ATM, accessible 24/7 for us to draw from its rich
resources whenever we have need. The biblical ATM does
not dispense psychology or motivational bullet points. It
dispenses truth.

Most modern believers don't realize they have access to
this line of truth. And of those that do, many have lost their

password. No wonder we're overloaded! We're attempting to live life out of the change in our pockets rather than drawing on the unlimited line of truth available to us at all times.

God created us. He designed us with a longing for deep happiness and true love. And he has told us how to live in order to find it. "The longing to be happy is a universal human experience, and it is good, not sinful," says John Piper.[7] The problem in our culture is not that we long for happiness, but that we have searched for it outside of God's good and gracious plan.

It is our contention that there are at least seven principles given to us by God that have been virtually abandoned among modern-day Christians. But these age-old principles enable us to overcome overload:

1. You need a Sabbath
2. You need a sanctuary
3. You need sustenance
4. You need supplication
5. You need to simplify
6. You need a Sovereign
7. You need a Savior

In Matthew 11:28–30, Jesus invited us to overcome overload not by reading the latest bestselling book by a psychologist or attending a dynamic seminar put on by a famous motivational speaker. He invited us to Himself:

"Come to Me, all who are weary and heavy-laden, and I will give you rest. Take My yoke upon you and learn from Me, for I am gentle and humble in heart, and you will find rest for your souls. For My yoke is easy and My burden is light."

Eugene Peterson, in his contemporary English version of the New Testament captures the gist of what Jesus was saying in this way:

"Are you tired? Worn out? Burned out on religion? Come to me. Get away with me and you'll recover your life. I'll show you how to take a real rest. Walk with me and work with me—watch how I do it. Learn the unforced rhythms of grace. I won't lay anything heavy or ill-fitting on you. Keep company with me and you'll learn to live freely and lightly." (The Message)

If I could offer the central idea of this book in twenty words or less, here's how I would do it:

Jesus knew how to live…and we don't.

That's why we're overloaded.

And that's why Jesus said, "Come to Me."

The very first step in overcoming overload is coming to Him and embracing Him as the sovereign God that He is. So let us begin.

Chapter Two

THE PAUSE THAT REFRESHES:
You Need a Sabbath

"Seven days without a Sabbath makes one weak."

BEN PATTERSON

IKNOWWHATYOURETHINKINGSOMEONE
MADEATERRIBLEMISTAKEINTHISPARAGRAPHIT
MUSTHAVEBEENTHEPRINTERORPERHAPSTHE
PROOFREADERBUTWHOEVERITWASSOME
ONEWASNTDOINGHISJOBHOWINTHEWORLD
DIDTHISPARAGRAPHMAKEITINTOTHISBOOK

I know what you're thinking. Someone made a terrible mistake in this paragraph. It must have been the printer, or perhaps the proofreader. But whoever it was, someone wasn't doing his job. How in the world did this paragraph make it into this book?

On the other hand, if you look carefully you will see that the two preceding paragraphs are identical—except for spacing, punctuation, and capitalization. I wanted to show you what written language looked like until about twelve hundred years ago. Until then, if you were reading a document in Latin or Greek, it would look like the paragraph you thought was a mistake.

For hundreds and hundreds of years, all writing was done in capital letters, *without punctuation or spaces between the words.* So it was hard work to figure out where one word came to an end and another began. But then, somewhere around the ninth century A.D., someone got the bright idea of putting spaces between the words to clearly separate them. And spaces made all the difference! Suddenly, reading got much easier.[8]

The Sabbath is God's space between the activity of life. It is God's way of ensuring that the days of our lives do not run together without a break. It's the space that protects us from the cumulative effects of living 24/7 lives. People who have not built a Sabbath into their lives are always running, working, pushing, producing—so they can keep on running, working, pushing, producing. In the end their lives become

- ruts without rhythm,
- regimen without refreshment,
- recreation without reverence.

Overloaded people need words that begin with "re." Words like *restore, revive, recover, recline, reflect, relax, replenish,* and *renew.* These words appeal to us because they seem so foreign to our daily experience. The first principle God has given to us for overcoming overload is the principle of the Sabbath. The Sabbath brings all these things into our lives—and more.

God created the world in six days and then rested on the seventh. He didn't rest because He was tired. He did it as an example for *us.* God gave us the Sabbath to protect us from overload. He designed it as a day to restore us—spiritually, mentally, emotionally, and physically.

People and nations observed the Sabbath for thousands of years, but more recently, the Western industrialized world has largely abandoned it. Even among churchgoers, the biblical idea of the Sabbath has become something strange and foreign. As the culture of 24/7, we know almost nothing about it.

And our ignorance is killing us.

Our lives have become like that paragraph with no spaces between the words. No commas or periods either—in fact, *no breaks of any kind whatsoever.*

You've heard of *TGIF* (Thank God It's Friday!). People used to toss that expression around in the 1950s and 1960s, back when workers actually took weekends off. But before that, for thousands of years people would say to one another,

"TGIS" (Thank God It's Sabbath!). And when they said "*Thank God!*" they actually meant it.

The Sabbath used to be the best day of the week. Now we don't even know what it is. Even Christians are confused. What *is* a Sabbath anyway? What should it look like? How should it fit into our modern lives?

Some think that the Sabbath is an Old Testament idea that has absolutely nothing to do with us today. Others were raised in families where the Sabbath was grim, ironclad, and strictly enforced—perhaps *too* strictly for anyone's good. No friends and no fun is all they remember.

But neither of these versions fits the biblical model. The true meaning of the Sabbath has become a well-kept secret.

DO YOU REMEMBER WHEN?

If you are at least fifty years old, you might remember a time when every store in town closed on Sunday. That was because of an unwritten law that said you simply did not make your employees work on the "day of rest." I remember as a kid when my mom would head for the grocery store on Saturday afternoon to get what we needed to tide us over until Monday. Every grocery store closed at 6 P.M. on Saturday. If you needed milk or sugar after six o'clock, you were out of luck, because everything shut down. You could borrow something from a neighbor, but you couldn't buy it at a store until Monday morning.

Why? Because Sunday was the Christian Sabbath. And, until about thirty years ago, America locked itself up tight on Sundays. Sunday was the space in the week that kept the other days from running together.

I grew up with grocery stores closed on Sunday.

My kids have grown up with grocery stores open 24/7.

And this cultural shift has changed the way we live. Our overwhelming concern for "progress and production" has squeezed out our God-given pause.

I had a real shock the other day. I was up at about 5:15 A.M. and realized we were out of coffee. So I jumped in the car and went to the store, where I almost bashed my head on the glass door. It didn't open! I looked up to see if I could spot the automatic sensor. Something was wrong. The door wasn't operating the way it normally did.

I was about to walk around to the other side when I noticed a new sign listing new hours for the store. I was shocked. That store had always been open 24/7. But no longer. Now they were closed from midnight until 6 A.M.

I must admit that I was taken aback. What was wrong with these people? Didn't they understand? I was out of *coffee!* And it was 5:15 A.M.! Why in the world didn't that store stay open?

I don't know their reasons, but I do know that it was a good experience for me. Like everyone else I know, I have become used to immediate access to whatever I want, whenever I want it. And frankly, I've been spoiled.

Now, I could have waited another forty-five minutes, but of course I was too busy. I also could have gone home and retrieved the used filter and grounds from the top of the trash can. Before 1950, some people didn't throw their coffee grounds away until they had been used at least twice. But it's hard to do that when you're used to a caramel macchiato with two shots of espresso, nonfat milk, and whipped cream on top.

"REMEMBER THE SABBATH...."

The Sabbath was intended to be a gift to us, not a punishment. It is a timeless gift, given by God. God created us with a built-in need for rest. He designed us so that we would need some space in our lives. Adam and Eve needed it—even in Paradise! And so do we.

But before we examine this gift, we need to do a quick flyover of the Sabbath and its place in Scripture. What does the Bible tell us about the Sabbath principle today?

As we track the Sabbath, we discover that it was intimately connected to four different people or events:

- Creation and the Sabbath
- Israel and the Sabbath
- Jesus and the Sabbath
- Resurrection and the Sabbath

Let's take them one by one.

Creation and the Sabbath

The Lord introduced the original concept of the Sabbath at the very beginning. God created the world in six days—and then rested on the seventh. The term *Sabbath* means "to cease" or "to desist from work or exertion." Genesis 2:1–3 states:

> Thus the heavens and the earth were completed, and all their hosts. By the seventh day God completed His work which He had done, and He rested on the seventh day from all His work which He had done. Then God *blessed the seventh day and sanctified it,* because in it He rested from all His work which God had created and made.

On the sixth day, when God created Adam, His work of creation was complete. When day seven rolled around, He rested. God then set aside the seventh day of each week as a day of rest: "God blessed the seventh day and sanctified it, because in it He rested." God the Father was teaching Adam a lesson by His own example. Adam was to work six days. But then, because he needed a rest—or a space, if you will—God set aside an entire day before Adam was to take up his work again. Adam needed a day to turn off his pager and not check his e-mail.

The Sabbath is right up there with the other timeless ordinances established by God at creation, such as marriage (see Genesis 1:28; 2:23, 24), child-bearing (see Genesis 1:28), sanctity of life (see Genesis 4:1–15), and work (see Genesis 2:15).

All of the creation ordinances were instituted before sin entered the world and before God gave the law to Moses at Sinai. And they continued to exist after the law was fulfilled by Jesus.

According to Bible scholar John Murray, "the creation ordinances of procreation, replenishing the earth, subduing the earth, dominion over the creatures, labor, marriage, and the Sabbath are not cancelled."[9]

It is interesting to note that each of these ordinances is actively opposed in our day.

- The ordinance of marriage is being challenged by those who want to make same-sex marriage legal.
- The ordinance of having children is opposed by zero population groups.
- The ordinance of work is rejected by those who desire a welfare state.
- The ordinance of subduing the earth (wisely using its resources) is resisted by radical environmentalists.
- The ordinance of man having dominance over animals is opposed by animal-rights groups.

The creation ordinances provide a blueprint for how we are to live. While it is true that sin came into the world when man fell, the fall has not erased these basic commands of God. If anything, the existence of sin makes them all the more indispensable. John Murray sums it up when he observes:

> These ordinances govern the life of man in that which is central in man's interest, life and occupation; they touch upon every area of life and behavior. The fall did bring revolutionary changes into man's life...but the basic structure of this earth, and of man's life in it, has not been destroyed.[10]

Israel and the Sabbath

The Sabbath next becomes an issue when the children of Israel escape the bondage of Egypt and begin their journey to the Promised Land. In the book of Exodus, God sets forth His plan and explains how the Israelites were to function as His people and nation. The Sabbath was a huge part of that plan.

First, God gave them a vivid illustration. When they were starving in the wilderness, God miraculously provided manna for them to eat (see Exodus 16). And that manna showed up, just like clockwork, for six days of each week. On each of those days, God had instructed them to gather one day's worth and no more. If they took more, it would spoil by the next day.

On the sixth day, however, just before the Sabbath, God told them to collect enough for *two* days. This extra manna miraculously lasted through the Sabbath and didn't spoil. God wanted them to rest on the seventh day, just as He had rested on the seventh day. Just to make sure they got the idea, the Israelites would wake up on the morning of the Sabbath to find the ground bare! The "grocery store" was closed! Anyone with any level of intelligence soon got the message.

Shortly after this, God gave the law to Moses at Mount Sinai. The Sabbath was number four in the Ten Commandments—the top ten rules for God's people.

> "Remember the sabbath day, to keep it holy. Six days you shall labor and do all your work, but the seventh day is a sabbath of the LORD your God; in it you shall not do any work, you or your son or your daughter, your male or your female servant or your cattle or your sojourner who stays with you." (Exodus 20:8–10)

Lastly, in Exodus 31, God made a covenant—an unbreakable, eternal agreement—with the Israelites. He promised that He would be their God and they would be His people. And the sign of that covenant was the Sabbath.

So what's the big deal about that? These people had been

slaves in Egypt for more than four hundred years. It was a brutal existence. God in His mercy delivered them through Moses. Once a week, the Sabbath was to be an ongoing reminder of God's mercy and provision.

The curse of slavery also shows up in the history of our own nation—and was a stench in the nostrils of God. Some of those slave owners were certainly what we would call brutal, heartless men. Yet, oddly enough, even the very worst of them gave his slaves a day of rest on the Sabbath. If he hadn't done so, the other slave owners would have ostracized him. Not letting a slave have a day of rest was considered a terrible violation. It simply wasn't done. It was inhumane.

We all thank God that slavery in our nation has gone with the wind. But isn't it ironic that, since that time, many of us in the land of the free have become even more enslaved to our work, our activities, and our "accomplishments"? We have become so chained, so utterly preoccupied, that we simply can't justify a day of rest. That, too, is inhumane. It's inhumane to your spouse, to your children, and to yourself.

Jesus and the Sabbath

Jesus was God's final word to us regarding the Sabbath. He interpreted God's design for the Sabbath as it was meant to be from creation.

When Jesus came on the scene, the Sabbath had changed so much that Moses never would have recognized it. Jesus observed the Sabbath by worshiping in the synagogues and temple. He saw what the Pharisees had done to "His day," and it deeply disturbed Him. On six different occasions in the gospels, Jesus went head-to-head with Israel's religious elite over this issue. These six confrontations with the Pharisees read like a six-part miniseries. Here are the episodes:

1. Outrage over Organic Wheat (Mark 2:23–28)
2. Hand-to-Hand Combat (Mark 3:1–6)
3. Back-Breaking Healing (Luke 13:10–17)
4. Dropping the Dropsy (Luke 14:1–6)
5. Stirring Things Up (John 5:1–9)
6. Spit in the Eye (John 9:1–41)

In the first episode, the disciples picked a few stalks of grain to eat on the Sabbath—our equivalent of putting a meal on the table. In the other five, Jesus purposely healed a suffering person on the Sabbath in front of the Pharisees. What wonderful, life-changing miracles! But did the Pharisees rejoice? Did they give glory to God? Of course not! They had laws against such things. And they cared more about their man-made rules than they did for suffering people.

In Mark 2:27–28 we read the bold statement that Jesus made to the Pharisees about their burdensome laws:

"The Sabbath was made for man, and not man for the Sabbath. So the Son of Man is Lord even of the Sabbath."

Clear as clear, isn't it?

It's important to remember that Jesus *invented* the Sabbath. Jesus created all things (see Colossians 1:16), including the Sabbath. And He is Lord of the Sabbath. The Pharisees had taken His Sabbath and loaded it up with more than 1,500 nitpicky rules and regulations. They had absolutely no right to do that. They took a good gift from God and made it into an unbearable burden for people to live under. Jesus took them on because they had almost ruined it.

But did Jesus do away with the Sabbath? Not at all! He did away with their baseless *traditions*—and that's why they hated Him. As J. C. Ryle observed, Jesus "no more abolishes the Sabbath, than a man destroys a house when he cleans off the moss or weeds from its roof."

Resurrection and the Sabbath

The final observation about the Sabbath comes after the resurrection of Jesus. Prior to that time, His disciples observed the Sabbath on Saturday, as did all Jews. But Jesus rose from the dead on a Sunday. And very early on in the life of the church, a significant shift occurred: the disciples began honoring Sunday *instead of* Saturday.

> The biblical evidence seems clear that the infant church in the New Testament held Sunday in great honor. Our Lord rose on the first day. Many of his post-resurrection appearances to various witnesses also occurred on Sundays. After the Resurrection, in striking contrast to their previous practice, Jesus' disciples habitually met and worshipped on the first day of the week.[11]

R. T. Beckwith summarizes the shift well:

> It is a striking fact that the Jewish Sabbath almost disappears from recorded Christian practice after Christ's resurrection. The very day before his resurrection occurs, we find the disciples resting on the Jewish Sabbath (Luke 23:56; cp. also Mark 16:1; John 19:42), but after it has happened, the observance of the seventh day is never mentioned except as a tolerated option for Jewish Christians (Romans 14:5)...or in passages where Paul reasons with Jews in the synagogue on the Sabbath (Acts 13:14, 42, 44; 17:2; 18:4;

cp. also Acts 16:13), not apparently because the observance of the day is a regular part of his own devotional practice but because it provides an excellent opportunity for evangelism.[12]

From Saturday to Sunday. In essence, that's what took place when Jesus rose from the dead. The emphasis shifted from the last day of the week to the first.

THE SABBATH SET FREE

Did the concept of a day of rest get downgraded or set aside after the resurrection of Jesus? No. And the reason is simple: The Sabbath existed from creation. As we have seen, God instituted it before the law was ever given.

That's why the concept of the Sabbath is still alive and well.

Jesus, however, sparked a change in thinking about the concept of Sabbath. Dr. James Stifler gets to the bottom line very quickly:

There is a Sabbath and it is divinely instituted in Mark, chapter 2. But there is not a line nor a word in the New Testament about how it is to be observed.[13]

Jesus set the Sabbath free.

In other words, Jesus liberated the Sabbath from the

1,500 rules and regulations of the Pharisees. And He went a step further. Because He fulfilled the law and offered up Himself as the Lamb of God—the final sacrifice for sin—we obviously don't make sacrifices anymore. Our observation of the Sabbath, then, looks very different from that of the Jews in the Old Testament.

Jesus underscored an abiding principle in His teaching: *the principle of worship and rest.*

Does it make sense that we need such a day at least once a week? Of course it does. God could have created the world in six nanoseconds. But He created the world in six days and rested on the seventh. God sanctified the Sabbath day for our benefit. If Adam needed a rest, how much more so do those of us who are slugging it out in this fallen world!

William Biloxi observed that "the Sabbath is God's special present to the working man. And one of its chief objects is to prolong his life. The savings bank of human existence is a weekly Sabbath."

The Sabbath is given for us to use each and every week. Not once a month or once a quarter or once a year. But once a week.

THREE SABBATH GIFTS

When we make the commitment to build a Sabbath in our lives, at least three gifts arrive on our doorstep:

- the gift of *rhythm* in life,
- the gift of *refreshment* in life,
- the gift of *reverence* regarding life.

The First Gift: The Rhythm of the Sabbath

There's an old song with the title, "I've Got Rhythm."

How about you? Is there any rhythm to your week? A life without rhythm turns into a rut. And the rut can get so deep that it can trap you and stall out your engine.

God doesn't want you in a rut. He designed you to live in rhythm. In fact, by His very design of the universe, God has literally "forced" certain rhythms into our lives. Every twenty-four hours the sun comes up and goes down. Every year has its seasons; summer, autumn, winter, and spring are part of the constant rhythm of life on Earth.

A woman has natural hormonal rhythms, as does a man. Another rhythm flows through the stages of human development. Children begin at babyhood, progress through childhood, pass through adolescence, and finally—thank God—move into adulthood! But the rhythm is the same for all of us as we move from young adulthood to old age, until we finally reach death. It is inescapable.

A weekly Sabbath is one of the rhythms established by God. And it can no more be ignored than any of the other rhythms of life.

God created you and gave you an Owner's Manual. He

knows you cannot run 24/7. You weren't designed that way! Nothing can—not your car, not your cell phone, not the machines in your office.

Cars, copiers, cell phones, and jets all come with a clearly laid out maintenance schedule. It could just as easily be called a Sabbath schedule.

So why in the world do Christians think they don't need to follow their Manufacturer's recommendations? We need to be spiritually, emotionally, and physically retooled and recharged. It's all right there in our owner's manual—and has been since creation!

Do you have a Sabbath rhythm in your week?

The Second Gift: The Refreshment of the Sabbath

Over the years, Coca-Cola has had some great marketing campaigns. Back in 1929, the ad men came up with the phrase, "The pause that refreshes."

There is no better phrase to describe what the Sabbath was meant to be. If your Sabbath pause is not refreshing, something is wrong.

Exodus 23:12 clearly states one of the purposes of the Sabbath. It speaks of allowing both people and animals to "cease from labor" that they "may refresh themselves." The ancient Hebrew word for *refresh* also means "to breathe." "A man is refreshed when, having exhausted himself, he recovers his breath."[14]

Have you ever thought to yourself, in the middle of a stress-filled, nonstop week, *I just need some breathing room?* The Sabbath is a built-in breather.

In some ways, we need the "pause that refreshes" more now than in any previous generation. Why? Because technology is intruding into every crack and corner of our lives, and the overload it brings with it, when we can't leave it alone, is wearing us out. One wise sage has observed:

> In a very short time, information technology has spanned the world. This affects the nature of work and the rest of life for vast numbers of people...where is the workplace if we can be hooked up at home? What happens to the "working day" if we can log in at any time of the day or night and store what we have done for another time? The boundaries between work and home, work and leisure, are complexified.[15]

A Sabbath helps to draw that clear boundary between you and your work.

Consider the two aspects of refreshment that should be built into your Sabbath celebration: rest and recreation.

Refreshment Through Rest

Historically, people have always worked six days a week. Only in the last fifty years or so have we gone to a five-day workweek. But now we have taken those other two days and filled them up, too! We bring our briefcases and laptops home. In effect, our work goes with us wherever we go.

Beyond all that, we have all the chores at home that don't fit into our ten- to fourteen-hour workdays. These include mowing and weeding, washing and cleaning, plus taking the car in for its Sabbath oil change and the dog in for its bath (unless you do this yourself, which is usually a lot tougher than driving him across town!).

There are haircuts, faucet repairs, and bill paying. And then we have all our children's games to attend—the Friday night game, the early Saturday morning game, the afternoon or evening game, and then the Sunday game. Don't laugh! I know people who really do live like this. Oh…and did we mention the piano recital and the board meeting at church?

Where, I ask you, is the rest?

We're running just as fast on the weekends as we do during the week. Even going away for the weekend is a chore. There are so many cars on the road trying to get out of town that Friday afternoon traffic becomes Friday *evening* traffic.

The biblical idea of the Sabbath involves much more than just looking forward to the weekend. The idea in Scripture is that of *refreshment* and *rest*. God *rested* on the

Sabbath; He looked at His creation, saw that it was good, and gave Himself time to enjoy what He'd accomplished. That's the whole idea.

Lance Armstrong doesn't bike 24/7 when he competes in the Tour de France. He takes scheduled rests. Even in his prime, Michael Jordan seldom played four straight quarters of basketball without a rest. Hockey players and football players go hard, but they always go in shifts. Even marathoners take refreshment.

The Jews have understood this principle down through the centuries. Modern Israel is a remarkable land with a remarkable history. You can hike to the Engedi where David hid from Saul, or travel to Mount Carmel where the God of Elijah defeated the prophets of Baal, or sample water from the very spring where Gideon's men drank before they went into battle.

Just don't plan to go there on Saturday.

The whole country shuts down for the Jewish Sabbath. Every other day of the week, Ben Yehuda Street in Jerusalem is a happening place. But on the Sabbath it's like a ghost town. The entire nation inhales a national breath; they enjoy the pause that refreshes.

David Ford writes that the Jewish Sabbath affects the whole shape of life in Israel and is as imperative to the practicing Jew as work is. He says:

I remember a rabbi, in a television interview, being asked, "How have the Jews managed to preserve the Sabbath over thousands of years?" His reply was, "It is not the Jews who have preserved the Sabbath; the Sabbath has preserved the Jews."[16]

The Jews have this one right. The Sabbath is designed for rest.

C. H. Spurgeon gave some great advice to young ministers, but it applies to all of us. Take a moment to read his well-crafted thoughts on the need for Sabbath rest:

> Look at the mower in the summer's day. With so much to cut down before the sun sets, he pauses in his labor. Is he a sluggard? He looks for a stone and begins to draw it up and down his scythe, rink a tink, rink a tink, rink a tink. He's sharpening his blade. Is that idle music? Is he wasting precious moments? How much he might have mown while he was ringing out those notes on his blade. But he is sharpening his tool. And he will do far more, when once again he gives his strength to those long sweeps which lay the grass prostrate in rows before him. Even thus a little pause prepares the mind for greater service in a good cause.
>
> Fishermen must mend their nets and we must,

every now and then, repair our mental states and set our machinery in order for future service. It is wisdom to take occasional furloughs. In the long run, we shall do more by sometimes doing less.[17]

No one has said it better. Rest and reflection are both essential for the man or woman who would live a wise, rich, and purposeful life.

The Refreshment of Recreation

What renews and refreshes you?

The word *recreation* means to "re-create." We re-create when we get away from our work and enjoy life's blessings. Do you feel guilty when you cut loose and have fun? Do you feel that you should somehow still be accomplishing something? The same Creator who came up with *work* also came up with *recreation*! In fact, God literally *designed* us with a built-in need for recreation.

No one worked harder than the great Christian scholar, John Calvin. He was a disciplined man who was very serious about his work. But when Sunday came around, he enjoyed it to the max! After church on Sunday morning, Calvin could be found at the bowling alley. Well, technically, it was a bowling *green*. He loved the game of lawn bowling, and almost every Sunday afternoon he indulged his little hobby.

Calvin understood that a Sabbath rest could be found in

recreation as well. Maybe lawn bowling isn't your thing, but what *would* enable you to re-create and re-fresh? Playing flag football? Reading Louis L'Amour novels? Planting tomatoes? Wrestling with your kids? It's your call.

Let me urge you, however, to consider one more important thing as you re-create. Everything in our culture pulls families apart. Even when we are together we are not together. Parents are sitting on the sidelines; siblings are running in a hundred directions. Consider making a point of doing things together as a family on your Sabbath. Cook a meal or eat out together. Play in the yard or at a park together. Build something together. Watch a good video together.

Remember the old saying, "The family that prays together stays together"? You could also say the same of the family that *plays* together. Your children don't want your money (even though they may say they do!). They want you. And they will most remember the good times you have had together. Your spouse doesn't want your gifts. He or she wants your focused time and company. These are the things that can make or break a marriage and a family.

The problem with a guy who goes off hunting or golfing every Saturday and Sunday (if that is the *only* fun activity in his life) is that it completely omits his wife and children. Does that mean you should never golf or hunt? Of course not. We know a family of seven that golfs together almost every weekend. In fact, golfing has become their official family hobby. But that's exactly the point—it's a *family* outing. Think about taking along one of your children when you pursue your own particular form of recreation—or make sure you fit in some other time with these little ones. One day—and that day will come quickly—they will be gone.

Perhaps you resist the idea of a Sabbath. You're addicted to the rat race. You're fearful of letting go and letting down, even for one day. You may be thinking that a Sabbath is impossible for you and your family. If this is your thought, then the last gift of the Sabbath may help to bring you around.

The Third Gift: Reverence and the Sabbath

Reverence is the last Sabbath gift.

The Sabbath causes us to stop and look up.

It reminds us that we ultimately depend on God.

The Sabbath principle can be summed up in one sentence: "Seek first His kingdom and His righteousness, and all these things will be added to you" (Matthew 6:33).

The Sabbath is about honoring God first, at the outset of our week. It is a kind of tithe—a tithing of our *time* to the Lord. Tithing takes faith that God will provide. A guy without faith is not about to give any of his money to the Lord—especially if he's living from check to check every month! In the same way, a guy without faith is not about to give any of his time to the Lord. Not when his boss is looking over his shoulder and a promotion is pending. Not when there is so much to do and everyone else is working 24/7.

Taking a Sabbath involves a certain trust in the Lord. The Sabbath principle says that God deserves to be honored, that rest is essential, and that ultimately we rest in *His provision for us.*

The Sabbath is for refreshment. But it is also for the worship and reverence of God. We are not meant to recreate without reverence. Nor are we meant to live our Christian lives in spiritual isolation.

For thousands of years, the Sabbath day has included corporate worship—from the days of Moses all the way through the days of the early church. There is something about people gathering together to worship the Lord that brings about God's rightful honor and reverence in a nation. And there is also something about a family worshiping together with other like-minded families that speaks volumes to their children regarding the most important things in life.

In Hebrews 10:24–25, we are exhorted:

Let us consider how to stimulate one another to love and good deeds, *not forsaking our own assembling together, as is the habit of some,* but encouraging one another.

Consistent weekly worship with other believers is important to God. Yet in too many Christian homes, church attendance has taken a backseat to soccer, baseball, or the NFL.

What are we saying to our children when we forsake church week after week so they can play soccer, baseball, or football? Why would we forsake worship of the living God to embrace kicking a ball? Why not forsake soccer to let our children know who and what is most important in our lives? There is nothing wrong with sports. But when sport is valued over the worship of God, something is seriously wrong. All that we have comes from His hand. He deserves to be revered.

So many churches now have multiple service times that it has never been easier to worship with other believers. The only option used to be Sunday morning at eleven. But now, many churches offer additional Sunday morning services, as well as Saturday and Sunday evening services. Does it matter to God which one you attend? Of course not. Does it matter if you consistently don't attend? Yes, it does.

Let's not forsake worship. Let's not forsake the assembling of ourselves together.

THE SPIRIT OF THE SABBATH PRINCIPLE

Taking a Sabbath will set you apart in this world. It will involve making some changes in your life. It is a good gift from God designed to help you overcome overload.

But let's keep it as a good gift. Let's not make up our own Pharisaical laws, and judge our brothers and sisters because they don't follow our particular rules and preferences. The Sabbath is to be enjoyed and treasured. There must be latitude and freedom as to the *how,* the *what,* and even the *when* of the Sabbath. The heart of the Sabbath principle is that you take one regularly, and that it be a time of refreshment and worship. The God who sees all will notice that you are seeking Him first, and He will add "all these things...to you" (Matthew 6:33). Watch and see Him work.

People in every walk of life who love the Lord can implement a Sabbath into their lives. Some of you will have to become creative. That's good, because we worship a Creator who loves creativity. At times, doctors and nurses, pilots, athletes, traveling businessmen, and others have to find ways to creatively implement the Sabbath. A pastor must make a Sabbath of his own. Mothers with sick babies have to go with the flow and get creative. And their husbands, of course, also need to be sensitive to their wife's need for a Sabbath!

Some of you will decide to go to your employer and

request a Sabbath. Some of you will graciously make your commitment to a Sabbath clear when you interview for a job. You will be surprised at how many employers will respect such a request. It is a sign of stability, of character, and of refreshing personal values in a culture that has largely abandoned all three. Some of you will tell your kids' coaches that your children will not be able to participate in games that interfere with family worship. What you decide to do is between you and the Lord. But let me encourage you to act boldly in faith, knowing that He will honor your commitment to the Sabbath principle. I have seen God do some remarkable things for individuals who have done just that.

Are we bold enough to close down our laptops for a day?

Do we have the courage to forgo checking e-mail for twenty-four hours?

Do we have the discipline to let a few messages wait on our cell phones for a day?

Wouldn't that kind of commitment for twenty-four hours make a difference in our week?

You know that it would.

It comes down to this: Can you trust God enough to take a Sabbath off from work? Can you trust Him to provide for you?

Marva Dawn observes that when we truly implement the Sabbath:

On that day we do nothing to create our own way. We abstain from work, and our incessant need to produce and accomplish, from all the anxieties about how we can be successful in all that we have to do to get ahead. The result is that we let God be God in our lives.[18]

SUMMING UP

So how should you observe the Sabbath?

That's between you and the Lord. Remember, Jesus freed up the Sabbath from the rules and regulations of men. As a result, the way you observe the Sabbath could well be different from what some of your Christian friends do. In this chapter we've tried to give you a taste of what the Sabbath was intended to be. How you apply and enjoy the Sabbath is a matter of personal choice and conscience.

But more than anything else, the Sabbath was meant to be a day of rest. And there could be no better news to overloaded people.

When I was in elementary school, I took piano lessons for a year. That was it. I didn't do very well, but I endured, knowing that it would come to an end. I also endured several nerve-wracking recitals. I'd have to learn some piece, then play it in front of people. And I would almost get it...except for some little marks on the music that I always seemed to miss. One was squiggly. Another looked like a hat. And for whatever reason, I never saw them. I knew they were in there, but I'd forget.

And so I'd be fine until I came to those marks, and then I'd get into trouble. Because, you see, the marks I didn't see were called *rests*. And the composer had put them in so the performer would not play, but *rest*.

God has so ordained life that after every six measures, you're going to get a rest. You can do what I did and keep playing straight through 'em. And if you do, eventually somebody will get upset about it. It might be your wife, it might be your son or daughter, it might even be your cardiologist. And they'll point out to you that there's a *rest* there.

One fine day when I played that piece, for some reason I saw the sign for the rest and I rested. And when I got done, my piano teacher applauded.

It was John Ruskin who said:

Not without design does God write the music of our lives. Be it ours to learn the time and not be discouraged at the rests. They are not to be slurred over, not to be omitted, not to destroy the melody, not to change the keynote. If we look up, God Himself will beat the time for us. With the eye on Him, we shall strike the next note full and clear, because we rested.

It's the rests that make the difference in the music of our lives. They really are the pauses that refresh.

Chapter Three

SOLITARY REFINEMENT:
You Need a Sanctuary

"We need society, and we need solitude also, as we need summer and winter, day and night, exercise and rest."

PHILIP G. HAMERTON

T he Pacific ocean.
A quiet, secluded beach.
Sunset.

Waves crashing in upon the shore—one after the other after the other, their sound like a rhythmic oceanic heartbeat.

A soft breeze, ebbing and flowing in a tide of its own.

Seagulls encircling, dipping, resting.

A fading distant horizon, gently arched, hinting of infinity.

Prisms of color, refractions of the sky, shimmering like glass.

The sun, quietly slipping away, waning in brilliance, but promising to return.

What is it that draws us to such places? Why do we thirst for them? What is it about them that immediately lifts an invisible load off our shoulders? Is it the beauty, the *natural* beauty, that stretches out before us? The silence and solitude? The reminder of our minuteness, the sense of something vast and great beyond the world we humans have made for ourselves? The promise of tomorrow in the unending tides?

I think it is all these things. A secluded beach is a sanctuary, a place of refuge and protection. All of us need such a place, where the world is put right, where the infinite touches the finite. A place where you can clear your mind and think. A place with no human distractions, no cell phones or e-mails, no radios or televisions. A place where you can set aside the demands of life, if only for a moment.

There is no place quite like Hawaii. We had the privilege of traveling to the island of Maui. Maui forces you to relax. The speed limit is thirty-five mph. Every road has only two lanes, one coming and one going. The weather is perfect, and the beaches indescribable. What a paradise! What a sanctuary!

Yet Hawaiians are leaving these beautiful islands— including Maui—in droves. The cost of living is so astronomical that the average family can't afford to buy a home. The economic pressures are forcing them out of paradise. So where are these Hawaiians going? Would you believe Las Vegas? They are moving from a lush, green, tropical paradise to the brown desert of Nevada.

Las Vegas is now home to nearly sixty-five thousand Hawaiians. They have come to the desert because they can find more jobs, get better pay, and afford the housing. Even Hawaiians who don't move to Las Vegas love to visit. Hawaiians make over 300,000 trips a year to Las Vegas.[19] They have become so comfortable in the desert that many even hold their high school reunions there. Due to brutal economic realities, they have left the paradise of Hawaii for a better standard of living...in the desert.

Like the Hawaiians who can't afford to live in their own land, most of us cannot afford to visit the ocean with any kind of regularity. The rent is too high and the distance is too great. But you don't have to go to a beautiful beach or a rugged mountaintop—or even a vast forest—to find a sanctuary. A sanctuary can be found right where you live, no matter who you are or what your circumstances.

In fact, to overcome overload you *must* find a sanctuary.

How? Like so many Hawaiians, you must head for the desert.

Or to put it another way, you must choose to become a desert saint.

THE MINDSET OF A DESERT SAINT

David Wells got me on this idea of becoming a desert saint.
In his book, *No Place for Truth,* he wrote: "There is an
unbridgeable chasm between the world's moral and spiritual
values and God's. So we are called to be exiled from the
world."[20]

He's referring to passages like 1 Peter 1:1 and Hebrews
11:13. To be exiled from the world is to be different from
it, to carry a different set of values, to question its foundations, to think differently and live differently. David Wells
goes on:

> No matter how painful that exile may be, this is no
> easy antagonism. The deeper the chasm, the greater
> will be the need for the believer to develop *the charac-
> ter of a desert saint,* in order to preserve the vital moral
> and cognitive intellectual differences and to avoid
> accommodation.[21]

Accommodation to what? To the world system. To the
world's style of thinking, which is everywhere around us, so
pervasive and influential.

A desert saint. That's quite a picture, isn't it?

When you study church history, you find a lot of weirdness at certain times. Weirdness seems to hover around
Christianity. This is not because our faith is weird, but

because it is human nature to be fascinated by weirdness. It shouldn't surprise us, then, that Christians can take certain truths, completely skew the perspective, and run right off the map with them.

In the Middle Ages, one particular group tried to "get away from the world" by climbing three hundred feet up a mountain and staying there for fifteen, twenty, or twenty-five years. They did this because they thought they had to be cut off from the rest of the world before they could really know God.

They thought they were going to a sanctuary. But they forgot something. They still brought a part of the world with them—their own sinful natures! And nothing short of death can remove you from yourself.

God never suggests that we do such a thing. Jesus prayed for his disciples, "I do not ask You to take them *out of the world,* but to keep them from the evil one.... As You sent Me into the world, I also have sent them *into the world*" (John 17:15, 18).

What does it mean, then—in a balanced, healthy way— to be a desert saint?

The life of a desert saint is characterized by regular, purposeful withdrawal from the world (a Sabbath) to a desert place (a sanctuary). Why does he retreat to a sanctuary? He does it to derive his direction and sustenance from God. You cannot be different from the world if you never separate yourself from it. You cannot see the world objectively if you never purposely extricate yourself and look at it from afar. You cannot recognize the treachery of the world's system and its thinking if you never allow yourself to withdraw and hear from God.

We are not talking here about a family get-together. We're not talking about a church worship service, as important as that may be. We're not talking about being with some close friends in a small group. Many of these things can be part of a Sabbath. But in this chapter we're talking about a *particular kind of Sabbath*—a personal, regular resting in the Lord in a *particular kind of sanctuary*—that secret place where you and the Lord can meet, one-on-one. That's what we mean by a sanctuary.

In *The Still Hour,* Austin Phelps observes:

> It has been said that no great work in literature or in science was ever wrought by a man who did not love solitude. We may lay it down as an elemental principle of religion, that no large growth in holiness was ever gained by one who did not take time to be often long alone with God.

But in this day and age, how do we establish a personal sanctuary? Mothers of young children may want to laugh at the whole idea. *A sanctuary? In your dreams! Where could I find such a thing?* Fathers who drive to work in rush hour traffic every day and then come home to the demands of being a biblical husband and father may wonder, *Is this guy living in the real world?* Single parents who are attempting to be both father and mother might think, *I'm lucky if I can eat and sleep!*

Yet I would submit to you that the idea of a sanctuary is biblical. And it is essential to your life. Yes, the concept can seem totally contrary to our modern way of life. But let me ask you something. Is there anything biblical that *doesn't* in some way go against the grain? Let me assure you that it is possible to find a sanctuary in the most difficult circumstances. Even a prisoner can find a place of sanctuary.

I invite you, then, to look with me at some practical ways to discover that place of sanctuary within your own life.

THE SANCTUARY PRINCIPLE: ORDAINED BY GOD

The idea of a sanctuary was established by God in the Old Testament. It was the place where God established His presence, where the people could gather to worship Him. First, He established the tabernacle. Then, after David subdued most of Israel's enemies and solidified his leadership, God allowed Solomon, David's son, to build the original temple in Jerusalem. Hundreds of years later, Jesus Himself often went to the sanctuary in Jerusalem that existed then—not Solomon's original temple, but its successor.

But on the day of Pentecost, when the Holy Spirit came upon the early Christians in Jerusalem, there came a shift. The sanctuary was no longer a building. The sanctuary became the hearts of believers. In other words, we carry the sanctuary around with us, for it is our hearts. First Peter tells us that Jesus is the cornerstone of the living temple of His people: "You also, as living stones, are being built up as a spiritual house" (1 Peter 2:5).

This means that you and I can meet with Him, one-on-one.

We can have an ongoing personal relationship with Him. What an amazing shift from the days of tabernacle and temple worship! "Do you not know that *you* are a temple of God and that the Spirit of God dwells in you?" says Paul (1 Corinthians 3:16).

But what good is it to have God's Spirit dwelling within you if you never stop to spend time with Him—if you never hear Him speaking to you above the noise of the world? "Abide in Me," said Jesus (John 15:4). But abiding requires one-on-one time. Just as your marriage cannot survive without one-on-one time with your spouse and just as your children need a one-on-one relationship with you, so your spiritual life depends upon time spent alone with the Lord. Failing to visit the sanctuary ensures an eventual distancing from God and an unhealthy drawing near to the world.

And that, my friend, is a prescription for overload.

Your cell phone battery doesn't maintain power for three or four weeks, or six months, or a year. You have to recharge that battery. You have to plug it in. A sanctuary is a place where you recharge your batteries. It's a place where you reinvigorate your spirit.

What, then, does a sanctuary look like? A sanctuary has three main characteristics: *solitude, silence,* and *stillness.*

Solitude

Solitude involves a *cessation of human interaction.* We need a place where we can get alone. I like what Dallas Willard writes:

> In solitude we purposefully abstain from interaction with other human beings, denying ourselves companionship and all that comes from our conscious interaction with others. Solitude frees us, actually. This above all explains its priority among the spiritual disciplines. The normal course of day-to-day human interactions locks us into patterns of feeling and thought and action that are geared to a world set against God. Nothing but solitude can allow the development of a freedom from the ingrained behaviors that hinder our lives, according to God's life.[22]

Our world suffers from a herd mentality. We see it at Christmas when parents rush out to get the latest "hot" toy. We see it on Friday nights, when audiences pack out the latest "hot" movie. We see it in the investment world when everyone tries to buy the latest "hot" stock. There's nothing wrong with toys or movies or investments per se. But when we never separate ourselves long enough to look at the herd from afar, we can lose our perspective.

Running with the herd can be a dangerous activity. In his book, *Markets, Mobs, and Mayhem,* Robert Menschel writes:

A few years ago, the NASDAQ was flying high and dot-com millionaires were a dime a dozen. The American economy appeared to be riding an endless wave of soaring stock prices…. Television's talking heads said that nothing like the tech boom had ever happened before and that there was no reason to think it would ever end.

In fact, it was only the latest version of an important story: group hysteria. Ever since 1630s Holland became the center of a massive explosion in tulip speculation, bubbles and busts have shaped history—economically, socially, and politically. Today, with the scope of the media and the ease of obtaining information, we are more at risk than ever. Elections are won or lost on hype alone; scandal can go global in a matter of seconds on the Internet. Keeping your head has never been harder.[23]

Menschel is correct. When we find ourselves caught up in the herd and the panic of the moment, we can make poor decisions that have long-term consequences. As believers, we are to be *in* the herd but not *of* the herd. We don't take our cues from the herd; we take our instructions from the Great Shepherd.

Have you ever been around a herd of cattle? You don't have to be a cowboy to observe that when one steer gets spooked and starts to run, the whole herd takes off. You and I as believers are to be different from the herd. And to be different, we must purposefully step outside of it.

Jesus, our ultimate model, demonstrates that. Jesus never took His cues from the herd, but there was always a herd pursuing Him. Once when He was followed by five thousand men, along with their wives and children, Jesus sought solitude:

Immediately He made the disciples get into the boat and go ahead of Him to the other side, while He sent the crowds away. After He had sent the crowds away, He went up on the mountain by Himself to pray; and when it was evening, He was there alone. (Matthew 14:22–23)

Go over to Mark 1:35 and you see it again:

In the early morning, while it was still dark, Jesus got up, left the house, and went away to a secluded place, and was praying there.

Once again, Jesus withdrew from everyone—including His disciples. He had a work to do. He was active and involved. He was responsible. He was the Messiah. But He knew He couldn't do all that He needed to do without meeting alone with the Father.

Let me draw your attention to one more passage, Luke 4:42:

When day came, Jesus left and went to a secluded place; and the crowds were searching for Him, and came to Him and tried to keep Him from going away from them.

I really like that last verse. He departed and went to a lonely place, but the crowd ran after Him and searched for Him! If you are a mother of young children, you understand completely. You've tried to remove yourself momentarily, and they *still* manage to find you. Children are demanding. Their needs are great. As babies, they depend on Mom for their very food and drink. They are fragile physically and emotionally.

But the demands don't go away just because a child starts to walk or graduates from diapers. You're only getting started! They just change with each phase of their lives. As I said when we were talking about the Sabbath, children go through phases, and parents go through each phase with them. These are among the rhythms of life and cannot be escaped.

Everyone understands what it is to deal with the demands of life. There will always be people who have an agenda for your life. And some of these things are good and right. Others are unnecessary or low on the scale of importance. We can't do it all, but there are some things we *have* to do to keep our sanity, to keep our balance, to keep our equilibrium; and to keep truth, righteousness, and obedience in their proper places within our lives.

Solitude is one of those things. But the minute you seek it, they'll come after you!

That's why I love Mark 1:35.

What did Jesus do? He refused to be tyrannized by the immediate and the urgent. He knew that the needs of His disciples and the multitudes would always be there. He knew that even if He went 24/7, they would *still* beckon. So He had the wisdom to withdraw for a while. He knew that in withdrawing He was gaining perspective, which would then help Him deal with the demands before Him.

When we withdraw from the people in our lives, we can

think and see more clearly. We can discard the things that really aren't all that important, that don't really count. We can be renewed by being alone with our wise and sovereign Father.

"Learn to say no," Spurgeon once said. "It will do more good for you than learning to read Latin."

"Why would anyone want to read Latin?" you say. But in his day that was a big deal. We tend to make room for everything important except meeting with our Father. But you have to say no somewhere else before you can say yes to Him.

We will consider the "how" of all this in a moment. For now, it is important to simply realize that we can't live well without solitude.

Silence

Solitude is a cessation of human interaction. Silence is a *cessation of noise.*

Last summer we spent five days in New York City. We walked the streets and visited the harbor. And soon we began to realize something strange to us...there was no silence anywhere. None at all. We found no place for escape—not even in the elevator or hotel room. The noise was incessant and pervasive. It seemed there was no place that we could escape. It was as if the city were on top of you. I would take walks and seek out a tiny café somewhere, but the noise from the streets would still invade the space. We went to Central Park, hoping for a respite. But it wasn't quiet even in Central Park. Once we took a trip to the Empire State Building. It was almost midnight, with a clear moonlit sky. Stepping outside on the top floor into the fresh night air, we thought, *Maybe it will be quiet here.* But even at midnight, 102 stories and 1,250 feet up, the sounds of the busy city filled the air.

I think New York City is a picture of our modern lives. We simply weren't designed for constant noise. We have to have some silence or we will get overloaded. Jim Elliot said, "I think the devil has made it his business to monopolize on three elements. Noise, hurry, and crowds. Satan is quite aware of the power of silence."[24]

If there is always noise, always clamor, always the radio, the CD, the television, how will I ever hear the voice of God? Someone once said that God speaks loudest in the quiet place.

The Bible talks about silence. David says in Psalm 62:

My soul waits in silence for God only;
From Him is my salvation.
He only is my rock and my salvation,
My stronghold; I shall not be greatly shaken....
My soul, wait in silence for God only,
For my hope is from Him. (vv. 1–2, 5)

David was talking to himself, to his soul. He was quieting himself and forcing his soul to wait in silence before God. For those addicted to activity and noise, this might seem a difficult concept at first. After a few moments of silence, we may tend to run. After all, we've got too much to do! But the rewards are great for those who wait.

Lamentations 3:24–26 says this:

"The LORD is my portion," says my soul,
"Therefore I have hope in Him."
The LORD is good to those who wait for Him,
To the person who seeks Him.
It is good that he waits silently
For the salvation of the LORD.

Whenever I meet mature believers, I find that this is a part of their lives. Those whose roots go down deep into Christ have learned the value of solitude and silence. Donald Whitney says:

The discipline of silence is the voluntary and temporary abstention from speaking, so that certain spiritual goals might be sought. Sometimes silence is observed in order to read, write, and pray, and so on. Though there is no outward speaking, there are internal dialogues with self and with God. This can be called outward silence. Other times silence is maintained, not only outwardly, but also inwardly, so that God's voice might be heard more clearly…. Think of silence and solitude as being complimentary. Without silence and solitude, we become shallow…. Silence and solitude are usually found together…[but] Western culture conditions us to be comfortable with noise and crowds, not with silence and solitude.[25]

Have you ever been in a sound booth in a radio station? There is a radio station in Dallas that I have visited on a number of occasions. It's fronted by one of the busiest freeways you will ever see. Cars rush by, trucks blow their horns, emergency vehicles tear past with sirens wailing. You can hear all of this as you sit in the station's reception area.

But when you step into one of the soundproof studios, the penetrating and irritating noise of the freeway comes to an immediate halt. The door closes behind you with a distinctive whoosh, sealing off the studio. Heavy and thick, the door and walls are covered from floor to ceiling with foam material, shaped like egg cartons, that absorbs all outside sound.

When you walk into that studio and shut the door, the whoosh puts up an invisible barrier that sounds cannot penetrate…and silence takes over. The outside noise and influence of the world have been completely shut off. And the

only sound you will hear is what comes through your head-
phones.

So should it be in our sanctuary.

An old Bavarian proverb says: "With silence one irritates
the enemy." This is the value of silence. The whoosh of the
sealed door of our sanctuary shuts out the lies and influences
of the enemy. And in the silence we listen and hear the truth
of God.

Stillness

Stillness is the last characteristic of a sanctuary. Stillness is
the *cessation of activity*. It is the ceasing from all tasks, except
the one single task of meeting with God.

This one is especially hard for those of us who don't like
to sit still!

When our oldest daughter was in high school, she never
stopped until she hit the sheets at night. She went from
cheerleading to class to friends to every conceivable student
activity you could imagine. We got exhausted just watching
her. One summer she had a break of a few weeks with
absolutely nothing planned. No friends. No camp. No
school.

At the beginning of that break, she would sit down to
read and her foot would begin to twitch. You've seen that
unconscious, restless twitch people sometimes get when they
have to sit still. It took a full two weeks before that twitch

went away and she actually began to find the rest enjoyable.

Sometimes when we refuse to cease from activity on our own, God forces us to stop anyway.

The LORD is my shepherd,
I shall not want.
He *makes me to lie down* in green pastures;
He *leads me beside quiet waters.*
(Psalm 23:1–2)

Sometimes God puts us into a hospital bed.

Sometimes He puts us beside the hospital bed of another.

Sometimes He removes the obstacles we have used as an excuse for not resting, such as a job or a relationship.

But the best way to find stillness is simply to stop of our own volition and be still. "Be still [or cease striving], and know that I am God" (Psalm 46:10, NIV).

Let me pause here to draw a distinction between biblical solitude, silence, and stillness, and what we may find in various other religions of the world. We are not talking about the emptying of our brains, the shutting down of our minds, the bottling-up of our emotions, or any other kind of trancelike experience. God wants to engage us on every level, so the biblical form of solitude is vastly different from all that. The next two chapters of this book will make this clear. What we do and what we bring with us when we go to our sanctuary is of utmost importance, for it is there that we will eat and breathe spiritually. Listening to and communicating with God requires something of us. But in order to listen and communicate, we must first have a sanctuary.

So how do we establish one?

CLOSET CHRISTIANS

How do you find a sanctuary in your busy life, a place where you can meet with God in solitude, silence, and stillness? You can start by becoming a closet Christian.

There are various terms in the Bible for a personal sanctuary, but none are more visual than the one used by Jesus. "Go into your inner room" said Jesus, "close your door and pray to your Father who is in secret, and your Father who sees what is done in secret will reward you" (Matthew 6:6).

The old King James Version refers to that private, inner room as a closet. How do we find such a closet? It may take some creativity!

- Isaac's closet was a field. He "went out to meditate in the field toward evening" (Genesis 24:63).
- David's closet was sometimes a cave, and at other times it was his bed-chamber.
- Hezekiah turned in his bed with his face to the wall and made that his closet.

- The prophet Elijah had a small upper chamber in an older couple's home.
- Our Lord's closet was a mountain.
- Peter's closet was a housetop.

You must find your own closet, or sanctuary. If you are a mom, it may mean having your husband stay home with the kids and going out and sitting in a restaurant with a cup of coffee and your Bible—even if you can only do it once a week. Some mothers can grab only snatches of time in their day while a child naps or nurses, or in the very early or late hours of the day. No one has to be more creative than a mother. You have to seek diligently for such times and then be even more flexible if the baby decides to interrupt. But it will amaze you how much restoration you will find in developing such a sanctuary in your life. God knows a mother's needs. Ask Him to help you find creative ways to be with Him.

If you have an hour-long drive to work, your sanctuary may be your car.

You may not be able to read Scripture when you're behind the wheel, but you can stick in a cassette tape or a CD of the Bible and listen. And you can put passages of Scripture on a card near your steering wheel, where you can think about them and claim them as you drive and pray.

You may find that your lunch break at work is the best

time for you to be alone with God. Or you may simply shut the door of your office and make that your sanctuary. I know people who put on their tennis shoes and go for long walks with their Bible in hand. This is their sanctuary.

Every person's sanctuary will be a little bit different. But that's the beauty of knowing and walking with Christ. *He comes to us wherever we are.*

You may not be able to find complete silence. If you live in a place like New York City, you probably won't. But that's okay. Do the best you can, and God will honor your efforts. Soon you'll find that you are tuning out the din of the world and tuning in to the voice of God. It's the quietness of your heart that matters most.

A Refuge of Your Own

Martha Stewart has been a household name for years. But have you heard of Chris Madden? Chris is an interior designer in Rye, New York, who wrote a pictorial book called *A Room of Her Own,* which has taken off like a rocket. It's a book about creating a personal refuge space at home, and according to a recent feature in the *New York Times,* "it has touched a nerve among frazzled American women."[26]

As a result of the response to her book, Chris Madden…

is fast becoming a brand in every room of the house. Since that successful book five years ago, she has written a string of others describing how to attain a soothing, English-country look in the bedroom, living room, kitchen and bath. She has a weekly television program and a syndicated newspaper column that reaches millions...in the last two years, she has put her name on expensive-looking but affordable collections of comfortable furniture.[27]

Some business analysts are comparing Chris Madden to the young Martha Stewart of twenty years ago. But there is a difference, a major difference, between the two. According to the *Times* article:

She is not building a business around how women should entertain family and friends or manicure gardens, but around *how they should seek solace and solitude.* Ms. Madden is not selling *how to impress;* she is selling *how to decompress.*[28]

Chris Madden herself speaks to the unique niche she has found:

There wasn't anyone speaking to women's personal needs for a *sanctuary*...nor were there affordable, durable, stylish home furnishings available to make their homes a haven.[29]

Here is a woman who has struck a chord—designing sanctuaries for exhausted and worn-out women.

Everyone is looking for some kind of sanctuary. In the fast, never ending 24/7 pace of life, people are missing something—and what they are missing is silence and solitude.

Both men and women need their sanctuaries. For men it may not be a room with Chris Madden furniture. It may be a comfortable den or a duck blind or a wood shop with an old coffeepot on the bench.

We know one couple that shared the same sanctuary. They had a very comfortable home. But the sanctuary for both of them, believe it or not, was their garage.

It was just a normal American two-car garage. Only they never put their cars in it. There was a coffee pot, an old table, and plenty of extra chairs. And with the garage door open, they could look out on several heavily wooded open acres behind their home. Year-round, winter, spring, summer, or fall, early in the morning or late at night, if you drove down the rear alley you would see one of the Wilsons in their sanctuary.

That may not be what Chris Madden had in mind.

And I seriously doubt that Martha Stewart would approve.

But it works for them.

However, there is something infinitely more important

than designing a sanctuary. It's what you do in the sanctuary that makes it a meaningful place. It's not the sanctuary that provides rest, it's what takes place there. God has no objection to hanging out in a garage—or in a closet, for that matter.

He just wants to be where you are.

Chapter Four

REAL FOOD IN A FAST FOOD NATION:
You Need Sustenance

"The Bible will keep you from sin,
or sin will keep you from the Bible."

D. L. MOODY

A n elderly man lay still in his bed, his breathing labored and shallow. Death hovered near. Lapsing in and out of consciousness, he was barely aware of his surroundings.

Suddenly, something changed.

The old man sat bolt upright in his bed, nose in the air. An irresistible aroma had startled him back to life! He caught the distinct, unmistakable scent of fresh chocolate chip cookies.

Somehow, the old man found the strength to push back the covers, swing his legs over the edge of the bed, and follow that heavenly fragrance into the warm kitchen. There, before his amazed eyes, he faced a wondrous sight. The kitchen counters were piled high with plates of freshly baked chocolate chip cookies.

Was this heaven? With a trembling hand, he reached out to grab one. But halfway to his goal, a spatula descended on his hand with a loud smack.

"Don't you dare touch those," his wife said, "they're for the funeral."

That's harsh! Even so, there is no proof that the old fellow finally died of malnutrition!

When Howard Hughes died in 1981, he was one of the wealthiest men in the world. Hughes was cared for around the clock by fifteen personal attendants and three doctors. He had the best health care money could buy. *Yet he died of malnutrition.* He died a thin, dehydrated, emaciated old man despite his bodyguards and his millions.

How did this happen? Hughes refused food and water for fear that it would kill him. He was obsessed about "purity" in food and water. But he overlooked the fact that a person also dies when he gets no nourishment at all. Food and water are the sustenance of physical life.

The same is true of the spiritual life. You can't make it without food and water. This chapter is about the feeding and sustaining of the soul. If you wish to overcome overload, this may be the most important chapter you will read. Sustenance is truly a matter of life and death for you—and for your children.

The food of the Christian life is the Word of God, the Bible. Jesus said, "Man shall not live on bread alone, but on every word that proceeds out of the mouth of God" (Matthew 4:4).

In John 4:14, Jesus spoke to the woman at the well and told her, "Whoever drinks of the water that I will give him shall never thirst; but the water that I will give him will become in him a well of water springing up to eternal life."

Overloaded people are so busy that they sometimes go days and weeks without ever feeding from Christ in His Word. That's why such people tend to be spiritually malnourished. In fact, the reason they're overloaded is that they don't take in the daily sustenance they need to keep themselves going. William Gurnall once said, "The Christian is bred by the Word and must be fed by it."

America is a culture of fast food. We drive through and we take out. We eat as many meals in our cars as we do in our homes. One bestselling book coined the term *Fast Food Nation*. That's America, isn't it?

Fast food is quick and convenient. That's the upside. The downside is a little more serious. Our addiction to fast food is slowly starving us. We have become like Howard Hughes.

Surrounded by affluence and prosperity, we are slowly dying from malnutrition.

Now that can't really be true, can it?

Well, there are two kinds of physical starvation. The first kind of starvation comes from eating no food at all. This is sometimes called *hollow* starvation, because those who suffer from it feel the hollow pangs. We've all had our hearts broken by tragic pictures of men, women, and little children dying from this type of starvation.

In this chapter however, we'll concern ourselves with a second kind of starvation. This kind of starvation comes from eating the wrong kind of food. It is called *hidden* starvation, because it creeps up slowly, quietly breaking down the vital organs and systems of the body and weakening the immune system. Eventually, if left to itself, it kills.

Most of us have heard stories from previous centuries in which people died from hidden starvation. In our health classes we've heard about "conquered diseases" such as rickets (a calcium deficiency that destroys the bones), and pellagra (a niacin deficiency that prevents the metabolism of food). A more familiar but still not-so-modern disease might be scurvy. Scurvy was common among sailors living on sailing ships for months on end with no way to get any vitamin C. Their joints would swell, their teeth would fall out, and their organs would eventually shut down. That's not real pleasant to think about, is it?

The great explorer Vasco de Gama once lost 100 out of 160 men from scurvy on one voyage alone. It wasn't until the late 1700s that the British navy got the bright idea of putting their sailors on a daily ration of lime juice (hence the name *limeys*) to prevent the disease.[30]

But these diseases have been pretty much eliminated from the modern westernized world. So does this mean that malnutrition is a thing of the past? No. Sadly, far from it.

FIZZ AND FRENCH FRIES

Research now shows that the majority of Americans today are malnourished. But it's not because we're underfed. If anything, we're probably overfed. Our problem is *hidden* starvation; the foods we eat every day are actually killing us.

Let me give you an example. In the early 1900s, the average American ate less than a pound of sugar every year. Now the average American consumes 140 pounds of sugar in the same 365 days.

Twenty years ago the typical teenage boy drank about seven ounces of soda every day—and twice as much milk as soda. Today the ratio has been reversed, with boys drinking three times more soda than they did two decades ago. According to one study, a significant number of boys drink five or more cans of soda a day! And girls are right behind them. Some in the industry like to refer to our new choice of sustenance as "liquid candy," because a single can of soda contains about ten teaspoons of sugar.[31] Many children now suffer from a well-hidden but increasingly acute calcium deficiency.

How many French fries do you eat in a year? Forty years ago, we averaged four pounds of French fries per person each year. Now, the average American eats *thirty* pounds of French fries in the same time period.

It's no wonder that a recent study on eating patterns among Americans concluded that our way of life is related to our way of death.

The problem isn't just in what we're eating. It's also in what we are *not* eating. On any given day, 41 percent of Americans eat no fruit, 82 percent eat no cruciferous vegetables, 72 percent eat no vitamin C–rich fruits and vegetables, 80 percent are missing vitamin A–rich fruits or vegetables, and 84 percent eat no high-fiber grain food.[32] The very nutrients we need for restoring and strengthening our bodies, and arming our immune systems against disease, are completely missing from many of our diets. This combination of too much of the wrong things, complemented by not enough of the right things, has created epidemic proportions of degenerative diseases in this country.

So what does this have to do with overcoming overload? Everything!

Obviously, what we feed our bodies is important. But what we feed our *souls* is exceedingly *more* important. Jesus said to his disciples, "Do you not understand that everything that goes into the mouth passes into the stomach, and is eliminated? But the things that proceed out of the mouth come from the heart, and those defile the man. For out of the heart come evil thoughts, murders, adulteries, fornications, thefts, false witness, slanders. These are the things which defile the man" (Matthew 15:17–20).

Jesus was saying that, as careful as we need to be about what goes into our stomachs, we should pay *more* attention to what goes into our *hearts.*

Is it possible that you might be malnourished in a land of abundance?

How can a Christian become malnourished?

1. By feeding on the sugar-coated, mindless programming on television that mocks biblical values.
2. By craving the heart-clogging violence and sex of modern movies and seeing nothing wrong with putting such trash in one's mind. I read in the local newspaper this morning about the popularity of the latest James Bond movie among families. One father took his ten-year-old daughter with him to see it. Another dad took his eleven-year-old son. The last time I saw a James Bond movie, it wasn't Cinderella. Sex outside of marriage is celebrated, flaunted, and glorified. But according to these dads, it's no big

deal. Sadly, they're wrong. It is a big deal. That one father shouldn't be surprised in five years if his daughter turns up pregnant. After all, it's no big deal. But again, it is a big deal! Whether he realizes it or not, a father who takes a young son or daughter to a movie with this kind of sexual message is giving tacit approval to such behavior.

3. By allowing your children to play video games that celebrate killing police officers and blowing away other authority figures.

4. By giving your children unsupervised access to the Internet and chat rooms. If you do this, you're asking for trouble. You are literally "opening the door of your home" and inviting predators of all kinds to come inside and visit privately with your children. Only a malnourished father would do such a thing.

We live in a spiritual junk-food culture. Our courts work full-time to make sure that every message and every opinion, sound or otherwise, is given every opportunity to be heard. Yet there is no room for God. He is mocked on television, scorned in movies, blasphemed in music, and spat upon in the public school system. We move and live and breathe in a world that promotes "tolerance" but cannot tolerate the truth of the Word of God. And we are raising our children in this spiritually malnourished environment.

Something must be done or we will die from spiritual malnutrition. We have reached a critical stage. We must begin to feed our souls. And the only thing that will nourish our souls and the souls of our children is the Word of God.

May I ask you a pointed question?

How is your spiritual diet? What do you feed on? If you are not consistently feeding on the Word of God, you will not have the strength you need to win the spiritual battles you will face.

In fact, you will not stand.

SOUL FOOD

The Word of God has been called many things in Scripture. It is a living and powerful *two-edged sword* that pierces our souls (see Hebrews 4:12). It is like a *mirror* that reveals our true condition (see James 1:23), a *lamp* that leads us through the darkest hours (see Psalm 119:105), the *sword of the Spirit* that defends us in spiritual battle (see Ephesians 6:17), and the *rock* upon which a man and woman should build their house (see Matthew 7:24–27). It is also the *seed* that produces imperishable life (see 1 Peter 1:23–25) and abundant fruit here on earth (see Matthew 13:8).

But one of the most common descriptions of God's Word has to do with food. It is the *pure milk* by which we grow and taste the kindness of God (see 1 Peter 2:2–3). It is the *solid food* that makes us mature and trains us in good and evil (see Hebrews 5:14). It is *sweeter than honey* to our mouths (see Psalm 119:103), "more desirable than gold, yes, than much fine gold; sweeter also than honey and the drippings of the honeycomb" (Psalm 19:10). Jesus, who is the eternally existent Word, referred to himself as the *Bread of Life* and as *living water.*

God's Word is the organic, nutritious, delicious food of the soul. Yet although it is abundantly available to us, we still starve for lack of it.

This is a remarkable phenomenon. Consider the overwhelming number of versions of the Bible available to us today. Think of Christian radio programming, the vast array of Christian conferences, Christian bookstores in every mall, and booming mega-churches that seem to keep springing up every day.

Yet I would submit to you that the American evangelical church is dying of starvation. We have become the evangelical fast-food generation. We are building bigger churches than ever before. And yet in proportion to our numbers, we are reforming our culture far less. We are anemic and malnourished. And many of us don't know it.

What are we missing?

The answer is very simple.

We have forgotten our lunches.

When I was a kid in elementary school heading out the door to catch the bus, my mom would almost always say, "Don't forget your lunch!"

Why? Because she knew very well that if she didn't remind me, I *would* forget it. And if I didn't eat lunch, I would become tired, irritable, and sluggish. Being tired, irritable, and sluggish doesn't make for a productive day at school. When you're going to be at school for approximately eight hours, nourishment becomes an issue. If you eat a good lunch halfway through the day, you won't be as tired, irritable, and sluggish. And you won't be malnourished.

Many of us modern Christians have forgotten our spiritual lunches. That's why we're malnourished. And when you are spiritually malnourished in a culture full of junk food, it is easy—very easy—to get overloaded with things that *do not matter.*

In the Christian life, the Bible is your lunch. As we have already seen, it contains

- the Bread of Life,
- the meat of the Word,
- the milk of the Word,
- the honey of the Word.

In a previous chapter, we discussed the importance of finding a sanctuary. But there's something we failed to mention about going to the sanctuary. When you go to the sanctuary, you can't afford to forget your lunch.

America is the most productive agricultural nation in the world. Our grocery stores are stocked with every kind of fruit and vegetable imaginable. Never has such an abundance and variety of healthful, nutritious food been available. And yet in the midst of this great abundance, we give ourselves and our kids Dr. Pepper and French fries.

We do the same thing when it comes to spiritual food.

Never in the history of the world has a nation had such access to the Word of God. The average Christian home has several Bibles. Just a moment ago I walked among the bookshelves in my home office and in different rooms in our house. I counted thirty-two different Bibles.

That would have astonished young William Hunter. William Hunter was only fifteen years old when he was burned at the stake in 1555. William had a great hunger for Jesus Christ and a powerful desire to know His Word. But in the England of 1555, ordinary people were not allowed to have Bibles. The priests withheld the Scriptures from "commoners." Other than the Bible chained to the altar at the church, there wasn't a single copy of the Scriptures in William's village. Here was a young teenage boy who would have given anything to have just one Bible. But the Roman Catholic church didn't want people reading the Bible. As you might expect, this was a time of great spiritual darkness in England. Whenever the Bible is withheld, there is darkness. And where there is spiritual darkness, people die from malnutrition of the soul.

So why was William Hunter burned at the stake? William was so hungry to read the Bible that he walked into a church, opened the pages of the chained Bible, and began to read. An official of the church walked in and scolded him for having the gall to read the Bible by himself. Shortly thereafter, a warrant for his arrest was issued and he was taken from his family, wrapped in chains, and thrown into a dungeon for nine months.

He was then put on trial and given the opportunity to recant his evil deed—daring to read the Bible. The bishop offered him forty pounds and enough capital to start his own business if he would recant. William refused, knowing full well that he would die in the fire.

As he was chained to the stake, with the dry wood all around him, he was again given a chance to recant. Again he refused. And then he turned to the crowd and asked them to pray for him.

A judge called out to him, "Pray for thee? I will no more pray for thee than I would pray for a dog."[33]

The fire was then lit and the flames engulfed the brave young man. His last words were, "Lord Jesus, receive my spirit."

William Hunter was willing to die for the opportunity

to simply read the Word of God. Young William could not even conceive of the possibility of owning his own personal Bible. But what would have shocked young William more than anything else would be that a modern Christian could own a Bible—even two or three—and have complete freedom to read it, but not take advantage of such a great opportunity.

Yet that's precisely what many of us have done.

HUNGRY IN THE DARK

Overloaded people tend to be spiritually malnourished. We become malnourished when we do not consistently feed on God's Word. When we don't eat the good diet of Scripture, we are not only malnourished, but "in the dark" as well.

"Your word is a *lamp* to my feet and a *light* to my path" (Psalm 119:105).

When it's dark, you need a lamp and a light.

When you ignore the Bible, life gets dark…and you begin to make bad decisions. Why? Because life without the light of God's Word will result in a series of bad decisions. In a dark culture, the more you know the Bible, the better off you will be. Psalm 119—the psalm from which I quoted a few lines back—is the longest psalm in the Bible. That's a piece of information you may want to remember. It very well could save your life.

During a time of great persecution in England, George

Wishart, a local chaplain, was sentenced to the gallows for his faith. As he approached the rope that would take him home, his executioners extended a courtesy. It was then the custom to allow the condemned man to request that a psalm be read to all who were gathered to watch him die. Wishart requested Psalm 119. Psalm 119 contains 176 verses. That's a lot of verses.

As the minister was reading to the condemned man and the gathered crowd, he was almost to verse 120 when all in attendance heard the distant pounding of horse hooves. The horseman carried a message from the king himself—a pardon for George Wishart. Psalm 119 literally saved the condemned man's life.

Wishart was not the first man whose life was saved by this psalm.

Psalm 119 is a psalm about the Word of God. Did you know that you cannot live without the Bible? To quote Deuteronomy 32:47, "it is not an idle word for you; indeed it is your life."

In spiritual terms, America is becoming increasingly dark. We are snuffing out the light of God's Word all around us. This is why husbands and wives are divorcing, it's why children are neglected, it's why possessions possess us, and it's why our laws are ignored and flaunted.

Many of us grieve because Bible reading and prayer have been taken out of our schools. But may I ask you a question?

Has Bible reading and prayer been taken out of your home?

It is a remarkable fact that many Christian people who revere the Bible never read or study it. And when we don't feed on our Bibles, we get malnourished and find ourselves groping in darkness—just like everyone around us who doesn't know Christ. We begin to believe the lies of the world system. We make decisions according to what everyone else is doing rather than passing them through the grid of God's truth.

As a result, we find ourselves overwhelmed and overloaded.

In the remainder of this chapter, I want to briefly introduce you to four remarkable people. These four people all lived in the dark. They lived in cultures where the Bible was absent. As a result, individuals and families were severely malnourished. Yet God used each of these four individuals to make a huge difference and impact in their respective worlds.

What these four individuals had in common was their commitment to the Word of God—a commitment that shaped not only their lives, but the lives of countless multitudes.

JOSIAH, KING OF JUDAH

Josiah was crowned king when he was just eight years old. Do you have an eight-year-old? Can you imagine him as king of a nation? That's what happened to Josiah. He grew to be the greatest king in the Old Testament.

His story is found in 2 Kings 22–23 and 2 Chronicles 34–35. Josiah became king during the darkest days of Judah. It was dark because of the sin of Josiah's grandfather, Manasseh. Manasseh was the most wicked king in the history of Judah—the exact opposite of his grandson. Late in life he turned to the Lord. But the consequences of the damage he had already done to the nation were irreversible. The nation would never fully recover from the wickedness of Manasseh. He led the people into immoral sexual practices, the killing of the prophets, and the sacrificing of children to demonic idols.

After he died, his son, Amon, took the throne. The Bible tells us that Amon "multiplied guilt" (2 Chronicles 33:23). Amon did not learn from his father's repentance, but multiplied the earlier sins of his father. Amon ruled for only two years, and then he was assassinated. That's why his son, Josiah, took the throne at such a tender age.

In the midst of great spiritual darkness, God used Josiah to return the people to His Word. Josiah was truly one of a kind. He skipped over two generations and followed in the footsteps of his great-grandfather Hezekiah. It was said of Josiah that "he did right in the sight of the LORD, and walked in the ways of his father David and did not turn aside to the right or to the left" (2 Chronicles 34:2). Josiah was David's great, great, great, great, great, great, great, great, great, great, great, great-grandson. In case you lost count, he was separated from David by fourteen generations. But like David, he was a man after God's own heart.

At the age of twenty, he demonstrated his love for the Lord by completely obliterating idol worship in Judah. And I use that word on purpose, for he literally *obliterated* the idols and their hilltop sites. When he was twenty-six, he commissioned a remodeling project for the temple. While the work was underway, the workers uncovered the Book of the Law in the temple. It could have been a portion of the Scriptures, containing at least the book of Deuteronomy, or it could have been a complete set of the writings of Moses, what we now know to be the first five books of the Bible.[34] Apparently, almost all the copies of the Word of God had been destroyed under the rule of Manasseh and Amon.[35] In other words, King Josiah knew of no other copies of the Scriptures in all the land. So this was an amazing discovery!

Young Josiah had never read the Word of God in his life. This is why there was such great darkness before he came to the throne. The light of the Word of God had gone out in Judah, and the people were malnourished. But rediscovering the Scriptures changed everything.

When Josiah read them, he realized how far the nation had departed from God's Word. He immediately instituted reforms to bring the people back to obedience. Because of

Josiah's wholehearted obedience to the Word of God, God decreed that judgment on the nation would not come in Josiah's lifetime. Josiah ruled for thirty-one years, and when he died, God stated this about the young king:

> Before him there was no king like him who turned to the LORD with all his heart and with all his soul and with all his might, according to all the law of Moses; nor did any like him arise after him. (2 Kings 23:25)

Josiah was the greatest king in the Old Testament. No other king followed God with as unwavering a heart. God used him to bring light into a deep and profound darkness. The greatest day of his life was that day when the temple workers rediscovered the Word of God.

Have you made that same discovery?

Has the Word of God set you free from the darkness surrounding you?

Let's jump ahead to England, about two thousand years later, to another season of great darkness.

WILLIAM TYNDALE

William Tyndale was born in A.D. 1494, near the middle of the Dark Ages. The times were dark because the Scriptures had long been kept from the people by the Roman Catholic Church. Church leaders believed that only members of the clergy should read the Scriptures. For that reason, the Word of God was neither taught nor made available.

William Tyndale devoted his life to changing all that. Tyndale built on the work of John Wycliffe, a man who died a hundred years before Tyndale was born. Wycliffe risked his life on a daily basis to translate the Bible from Latin into English, then to have handwritten copies distributed to the people. Wycliffe was so hated for making the Bible available that "several decades after he died, they condemned him for heresy, dug up his body, burned it, and threw his ashes into the Swift River."[36]

Satan is not pleased when men and women gain access to the lamp and light of the truth.

William Tyndale built on the foundation Wycliffe laid down, except that Tyndale bypassed the Latin version entirely and translated the Scriptures from the original Hebrew and Greek, directly into English. Because his work was so violently opposed in England, the land of his birth, he fled to Germany. In answering a priest who criticized his work, Tyndale said, "If God spare my life, ere many years, I will cause a boy that drives a plow to know more of the Scripture than you do."[37]

The people did not know the Scriptures, but neither did the priests. Most of them were ignorant of the Bible. Their source of "truth" was the Pope.

One bishop in Tyndale's time did a survey of the 311

priests in his diocese.[38] One hundred sixty-eight of the priests couldn't repeat the Ten Commandments. Thirty-one of the 168 had no idea where in the Bible the Ten Commandments could be found. Forty could not locate the Lord's prayer. But here's the topper. Thirty-one of the forty could not name the author of the Lord's prayer. That's what you call ignorance. They couldn't figure out that the Lord's prayer was uttered by the Lord. No wonder England was in such darkness. And no wonder what Tyndale did was so risky.

When Tyndale completed his translation of the New Testament in 1525, more than fifteen thousand copies were smuggled back into England over the next five years. Officials did their best to stop the distribution. They delighted in burning Bibles whenever they discovered any.[39]

In May of 1535, Tyndale was finally captured and thrown into prison. Approximately one year later, he was burned at the stake. And why was he burned in the flames? Because he was committed to the idea that average people should be able to read the Bible. That was his crime.

Before he died, he cried out a loud prayer to almighty God that everyone heard: "Lord! Open the King of England's eyes!"

Little did he know how quickly that prayer would be answered.

HENRY VIII

If you are old enough to remember the '60s, then you recall a rock group called Herman's Hermits. One of their hit songs was titled "Henry the Eighth." Henry VIII is without a doubt the best known of the British kings because of his many wives. King Henry went through wives the way some men go through cars. Every few years he would get rid of one and find a new one. He was particularly upset when a wife couldn't give him a son. Eventually he would move on to another wife in the hope of having a son.

One year after Tyndale uttered his prayer to the Lord, a son was born to Henry VIII and his third wife, Jane Seymour. The baby boy was named Edward VI. No one suspected that this baby boy, who would one day be king of England, would be the answer to Tyndale's prayer.

Henry VIII is a historical enigma. He did some terrible things, but he also did some good things. And one of those good things was to provide some godly tutors to his young son, Edward. Through the efforts of two Protestant tutors, young Edward was steeped in the Word of God.

Sir John Cheke served not only as a tutor, but as a father figure and friend to the young boy.[40] Because of the unique relationship between the mentor and the young king, Edward flourished beyond his years. His maturity as a boy was shocking to the adults around him. He had remarkable presence and discernment. He also had a great love for Jesus Christ.

Henry VIII died on January 28, 1547. At the age of nine, young Edward became king of England. At his coronation, three swords were presented to him as symbols of the three kingdoms he would rule over. The nine-year-old boy-king then called out, "There is a sword that is wanting [missing]." There was a stilled hush as the officials looked at each other, not understanding what the young king was talking about. When they finally asked him what sword was missing, the boy replied, "The Bible."

Then he addressed the adults surrounding him:

That Book is the sword of the Spirit, and to be preferred before these three swords.... Without that sword we are nothing, we can do nothing, we have not power. From the Bible we are what we are to this day. From it we receive whatsoever it is that we at present do assume.... Under the Bible, the Word of God, we ought to live, to fight, to govern the people and to perform all our affairs. From it alone we obtain all power, virtue, grace, salvation and whatsoever we have of divine strength.[41]

This was not your average nine-year-old boy. This was a boy wise beyond his years. This was a young man who loved God with all his body, soul, and spirit.

N. A. Woychuck has written a fascinating history of

Edward VI that is appropriately titled *The British Josiah.* In it, he tells of the spiritual impact that this young man had on a nation in spiritual darkness.

> During Edward VI's reign, great reforms were initiated and the moral corruption began to be checked. In the six short years of his reign, the nation had been revolutionized. The foundations for the enlargement of true Christianity in England *were laid in the encouragement given to the people to read, mark, learn and inwardly digest the Word of God.*

They were taught that the gospel has God for its author, salvation for its end, and truth, without any mixture of error, for its matter. He sought to instruct his sister, Mary, who scornfully rejected his counsel. He did, however, help his sister Elizabeth, who followed Queen Mary, as the English monarch in whose reign Protestantism was resumed and more fully established in England."[42]

Young King Edward VI died at the age of fifteen. But he left his mark. He loved the Word of God, and he opened it to his people. He encouraged them "to read, mark, and inwardly digest the Word of God." What a legacy. He established a foundation for bringing England out of spiritual darkness by daring to love the Word of God.

On the king's death, John Calvin proclaimed, "Most

truly do you say, that the land has been deprived of an incomparable treasure. Indeed, I consider that, by the death of one youth, the whole nation has bereaved of the best of fathers."[43]

John Knox, the fiery preacher who turned Scotland upside down for God, said that Edward VI was the "most godly and virtuous king that has every been known to have reigned in England."[44]

Now what does this have to do with us?

First of all, knowing this bit of history should cause us to be very thankful to God that we have the freedom to read the Bible. Having unlimited access to the Word of God, without fear of death or reprisal, is a rare occurrence in history. If you pick up your Bible, you will not be reported to the authorities and burned in the fire.

Second, we should thank God for the brave men and women who gave their lives for the Word of God. Their bravery and courage should cause us to value our Bibles more than we ever have before. When Edward VI died, his sister Mary became queen. She did not share his beliefs. And during her short reign she became known as "Bloody Mary." She burned 288 men, women, and children at the stake, people who simply loved the Bible and Christ Jesus. One of them was William Hunter, the young boy we met earlier.

Third, we should be motivated to read our Bibles so that

we would not be malnourished. Quite frankly, many of us have neglected the Word of God. We don't value it as a great treasure. But it is the greatest of all treasures. It is our food and drink. It is our life. It brings us out of darkness the moment we read its truth. When the short reign of Mary was over, her sister Elizabeth took the throne. Elizabeth had been greatly influenced by her brother, Edward VI. She too, loved Christ and His Word. Elizabeth immediately began releasing prisoners that Mary had in chains. Following her coronation, some lords came to her and said, "There are four or five others to be freed."

"Who are they?" she asked.

"Matthew, Mark, Luke, John, and Paul," was the answer.

Elizabeth indeed set free the Scriptures. Before her reign was over, 216 editions of the Bible were issued from the presses.[45]

Matthew, Mark, Luke, John, and Paul have been set free in our day. And as we read their God-inspired writings, along with the rest of God's Word, it shines light into the darkness of our lives.

So how do you get started? There are many ways to begin. You can obtain *The One Year Bible*. It will enable you to read the Scriptures in a year by taking fifteen or twenty minutes each day.

If you are in your car or exercising at the gym, you can listen to the Bible on CD. You can download several versions of the Scriptures onto your palmtop and carry it in a shirt pocket or purse.

Isn't it ironic that we have more Bibles and biblical study materials available to us than at any other time in history, yet so few of us take the time to read the Book that gives us spiritual life?

In an age where our local grocery store contains scores of fruits and vegetables, we go through the drive through to get a Coke and French fries.

Are you tired of the frantic pace set for us by the prince of darkness? Are you tired of scrambling in the dark for wisdom and perspective?

Open your Bible. Read it. Make notes in it. Go to a church where it is preached without apology. Read it to your children.

Be a Josiah.

Be a Tyndale for your family and get the Word of God into them. And while you're at it, ask God to give them a love for the Scriptures like Edward VI had. Then they will have a lamp and a light that will guide them through the darkness for all the days of their lives.

Chapter Five

DECOMPRESSION CHAMBER:
You Need Supplication

*"Prayer is the Christian's vital breath, the
Christian's native air."*

JAMES MONTGOMERY

*"I pray on the principle that wine
knocks the cork out of the bottle.
There is an inward fermentation, and there must be a vent."*

HENRY WARD BEECHER

On May 23, 1939, Joe DiMaggio of the New York Yankees was about to claim his first major-league batting title. Bloomingdale's department store was promoting a new electronic wonder for American homes, called television. And Europe teetered on the brink of war.

But another less noted event occurred on that day. The Navy's newest fleet-type submarine, *Squalus,* went down off the New England coast in a training accident. She was state of the art and deadly. But now, at 300 feet below the waves, she had become a steel tomb.

Even if any crew members had somehow been able to escape the sub, the oxygen and nitrogen in their lungs would instantly turn toxic under the tremendous pressure of the water. They were more than one hundred feet beyond the lower limits—at two hundred feet, oxygen becomes fatally poisonous, and nitrogen enters the bloodstream and body tissues, causing an acute, often fatal decompression sickness also known as "the bends."

All on board the *Squalus* were helplessly trapped.

And they knew it well. From the time the U.S. Navy acquired its first submarine, the *Holland,* in 1900, everyone knew that there would be no deliverance if a sub went down in deep water. But on this day, for the first time, submariners had hope. It lay in a new invention called the "bell," and in its inventor, Charles Bowers Momsen.

You have probably never heard of Momsen, or "Swede" as his friends called him. But that name is revered among submariners. Momsen was a visionary scientist, a man of compassion and conceivably the greatest submariner in naval history. Momsen had his initial brush with death when his first submarine once plunged into mud, eventually breaking free. Later he survived a torrential hurricane in the Gulf of Mexico.

But the event that changed his life was the downing of a sister sub, the *S-51,* in 1925. Many of his best friends were on board, and all he could do was wait at the surface as they died below him, entombed under fifteen tons of oceanic pressure. On that day, Momsen determined to find a way for submariners to escape such a hellish end.

Everything that could possibly help to save a trapped submariner—smoke bombs, telephone marker buoys, new deep-sea diving techniques, escape hatches, and artificial lungs—was a direct result of Momsen's work. And now, after enduring eleven years of skepticism from his superiors, for the first time "Swede" was about to use his bell, a great pear-shaped rescue chamber he had invented for just such occasions.

Even in testing, the bell had never been this deep before. And so, for a half hour that seemed to go on forever, everyone waited topside with bated breath. When the first seven sailors were brought up safely, cheers erupted from the surrounding ships, and history was made. For the first time, men in a sunken submarine had returned to the surface alive.[46]

WHAT PRAYER IS TO BELIEVERS

That bell was to submariners what prayer is to believers.

They used to say, "If you want to teach a man to pray, send him to sea." Sometimes life can be like the ocean—placid one moment, treacherous the next. And sometimes the pressures of life can feel like fifteen tons. Evil overwhelms us. Circumstances press in. And the pressure threatens to crush us.

Prayer is the escape vehicle that lets you decompress from the pressures of life. It provides oxygen for the soul. Without it, your spiritual life will become cold and dead. Without it, you will eventually succumb, and "overload" will claim another victim.

A prayerless person is like someone who eats and sleeps but forgets to breathe! He is a person who does not *walk* with God. It is possible to build a certain rhythm into your life, rest regularly, get away to a sanctuary, read, and even *study* Scripture, yet never really pray. But if you do not pray, you have cut off your flow of oxygen, and the flame of your spiritual life will flicker, fade, and die.

Pastors, seminary students, and anyone else in ministry should take heed. Studying the Bible every day, parsing the Greek and translating the Hebrew, getting your theology straight—these are not guarantees against losing ground spiritually. In fact, sometimes we can be lulled into thinking all is well because we know certain Scriptures and have certain biblical principles under our belt. Sometimes we can think that in *doing the work* of the ministry we are *keeping alive spiritually*. But that is a lie. If you have sustenance without supplication, you are in trouble.

Prayer is to the believer what communication is to marriage. Without communication a man and woman soon become estranged from each other. Without prayer we soon grow estranged from God, and then it becomes easy for Satan to pick us off.

Beyond all that, when we spend time in prayer,

- faith moves into action,
- convictions turn into decisions to obey,
- we learn to trust the very word that we have put into our minds,
- we come to know God *experientially*,
- God works to bless us and change us.

That's why prayerless people are driven by the concerns of the world. They do not experience the benefits of depending on Him in the same way they depend on the air they breathe.

What do we mean when we speak of prayer? The title of this chapter uses the word *supplication*. I haven't included that term in my conversations lately, and I doubt that you have either. But it's a good term. The Bible uses it often. It means "a humble and earnest request." And that, in a nutshell, is what prayer is. Yet there is far more to supplication than first meets the eye.

DIVINE GENIE OR WISE FATHER?

Some Christians see prayer as a magic lamp and God as a divine genie. They view prayer as a means for getting what they want, a summons to God to move at their beck and call. You call it out, and He makes it happen—you speak what you want into existence. This is the attitude among certain groups of believers today.

But nothing could be further from what the Bible teaches about prayer. We pray because we have been instructed to pray. God does not recommend it. He commands it.

Cast your burden upon the LORD
    and He will sustain you. (Psalm 55:22)

Trust in Him at all times, O people;
    pour out your heart before Him." (Psalm 62:8)

"Pray, then, in this way: 'Our Father, who is in heaven…'" (Matthew 6:9)

Pray without ceasing. (1 Thessalonians 5:17)

Why does God command us to pray? Obviously, we are not praying to inform Him of our thoughts. He already knows our thoughts. We're not enlightening Him about our needs. He knows our needs—better than we do.

> For your Father knows what you need before you ask Him. (Matthew 6:8)

We are not changing His thinking toward us or persuading Him to change His mind. He is sovereign, as we will see in chapter 7. God already knows "the end from the beginning."

Why, then, does God command us to pray? Well, let's suppose you are in a rowboat, a mile or so from land. As you row back, it would be foolish for you to think that the land is coming towards you. The land isn't coming to you. You are going to the land. You can no more toss a hook and pull the land to you than you can inform or change the mind of God when you pray. What happens as you pray is that you pull closer to Him. And as you pull close to the Lord, He works in your life.

Prayer is for *our* benefit. Prayer is meant primarily to change *us*.

The primary purpose is to bow before the Lord. And when we bow before Him, the benefits flow back to us! As we pray,

- we mature (we gain faith and grow in our understanding of Him),
- we are humbled (we are reminded that He is great and we are not; He is holy and we are not; He is all-wise and we are not),
- we are blessed (God meets the needs we have laid before Him).

Remember the three lies of our culture? Prayer is the acknowledgment that we can't *have* it all, can't *do* it all, and don't *deserve* it all. Prayer says that we need God, that He is in charge. A praying person knows that his only true happiness comes from walking with God.

Now, if you don't believe that God is sovereign, you inherit a whole set of issues about prayer. A. W. Tozer once said, "The hard work of prayer is getting yourself into a state of mind in which you prefer the will of God over your own."

We have it reversed in the modern church. We get anxious and prescribe the answers, and when they don't come quickly, we decide that prayer doesn't work. God must not really answer prayer. He must not really work in people's lives ways that we can see, hear, taste, and feel.

Or we begin to emphasize our level of faith rather than God's level of wisdom. We decide that faith is measured by immediate, tangible, visible answers. If God doesn't answer our prayers, we haven't enough faith. But if that were true, why did some of the most mature believers in church history suffer and die for the sake of Christ?

John Bunyan understood the true purpose of prayer. Bunyan was imprisoned for most of his adult life. He could have walked free by agreeing not to preach the gospel, but he refused. So his family subsisted in poverty while he languished in prison.

Pilgrim's Progress, written during those years of imprisonment, is the number two bestselling book in the history of the world. (The first, of course, is the Bible.) Bunyan said, "If we have not quiet in our minds, outward comfort will do no more for us than a golden slipper on a gouty foot."

Bunyan lived on prayer. It was life to him. "The truths that I know best I have learned on my knees. I never know a thing well, 'til it is burned into my heart through prayer," he said, adding, "The best prayers have often more groans than words."

Prayer is essentially a child's groans and expressions to his Father. John Calvin said, "Prayer is ordained to this end that we should confess our needs to God, and bare our hearts to Him, as children lay their troubles in full confidence before their parents."

Do you remember how Jesus told us to pray? "Our *Father* who is in heaven, hallowed be Your name. Your kingdom come. Your will be done.... For Yours is the kingdom and the power and the glory forever" (Matthew 6:9–10, 13). We are to come to Him as His children, beseeching our Father. We are to begin by desiring His will. We are to continue by expressing our needs and requests. And we are to end by desiring His honor and glory.

I wish I had a nickel for every time one of our children would ask us for something and we would answer, "Not now." Or "No, honey, that would not be good for you." Or, "Wait until you're old enough." Yet they continued to come, and they continued to believe we loved them and would provide for them. They understood the concept of authority and wisdom. And they knew that if it was possible and if it was good for them, we would give them what they asked.

God is our Father, and He wants us to come to Him in the same spirit.

> If you then, being evil, know how to give good gifts to your children, how much more will your Father who is in heaven give what is good to those who ask Him! (Matthew 7:11)

The primary reason we pray is to grow close to our heavenly Father, who loves us and cares for us. "The whole meaning of prayer is that we may know God," said Oswald Chambers.

That's the "why." Now let us turn to the "how" of prayer.

THREE KINDS OF PRAYER

We are to pray in three ways. The first is *communal prayer*—the prayer which we express when we gather with other believers. The second is *concentrated private prayer*—that prayer which we offer up in our secret sanctuaries. The third is *continual prayer*—that prayer which you pray throughout the day as you go about your activities.

Communal Prayer

Churches in America used to hold three services each week. The first two were on Sunday morning and Sunday night, and the third was on Wednesday night. You might be too young to remember this, but I remember it well. Wednesday night was the midweek prayer meeting. Members would gather to pray about the concerns of the world, their community, and their people. This is biblical.

> Bless the LORD, all servants of the LORD, who serve by night in the house of the LORD! Lift up your hands to the sanctuary and bless the LORD. (Psalm 134:1–2)

> Therefore I want the men in every place to pray, lifting up holy hands, without wrath and dissension. (1 Timothy 2:8)

A nation characterized by such corporate prayer will be blessed by God.

[If] My people who are called by My name humble themselves and pray and seek My face and turn from their wicked ways, then I will hear from heaven, will forgive their sin and will heal their land. (2 Chronicles 7:14)

In spite of all these biblical admonitions and promised blessings, prayer can still seem like hard work at times—like digging a ditch with a toy shovel.

Do you find it so? Do you have a hard time getting your motor started in your private conversations with God? Do you get fidgety and find your mind wandering? I once had a seminary prof whose prayers alone made his class worth attending. When someone in class asked how he'd learned to pray, he said, "Well, my best praying was learned in the presence of like-minded believers."

Mary has discovered the same thing, as she relates the following story.

Mary, I have found that praying with a few close friends jump-starts my prayer life. There is something about close human fellowship that spurs me on in my private prayer life.

For the last two years I have met with a few close friends who are kindred spirits in the faith. One is thirty-something, another is forty-something, and I am fifty-something. Yet we share the same heart desires, and we find great encouragement when we gather to pray.

Once a week we have made it a priority to come together for about three hours. Nothing short of serious illness or extreme crisis has kept us from this time. We meet from 8 to 11 P.M., which sounds like a strange time but just happens to be the best time for us!

After many mistakes, our little group has learned what makes for the richest time in prayer. First we begin with Scripture. Either we read a particular passage or we focus on a particular teaching from the Bible. Once we took Martin Luther's little book, *A Simple Way to Pray*, and used it as a starting point. Luther was known to be a man of prayer. He once said, "I have so much to do that I spend several hours in prayer before I am able to do it."

Luther was asked by his barber if he could give him some tips on praying. "I have a difficult time when I go to pray," said the barber. So Luther wrote this little book for his barber. In it, Luther's main point is that we pray best when we pray straight out of Scripture. And that is what our group has discovered.

Have you ever prayed that way? You simply take a verse of Scripture that speaks to your heart, personalize it, and pray it right back to God. Let's say you'd been thinking about Romans 8:28. You might use that verse as a springboard to pray something like this: *Lord, I'm so encouraged that You cause all things to work together for good in my life because I love You. Thank You for calling me according to Your good purpose.*

Or maybe you could take Hebrews 13:5 and 8: *Lord Jesus, thank You that You have promised never to desert me and never forsake me. I praise You that You are the same yesterday, today, and forever.*

Many of the psalms are already highly personalized. Pray those words of passion, fear, loneliness, and praise right back to the Great Shepherd. *In you, O LORD, I have taken refuge; Let me never be ashamed* (see Psalm 31:1).

There is power and comfort in giving voice to God's own inspired word, and sending it back to heaven where it came from!

The second thing we do is share personal requests. This is a time of great encouragement, because we are unburdening our hearts with wise, trusted friends. We write down our requests for one another, our spouses and children, our nation, and anyone or anything else that comes especially to mind.

Then we pray. It's sometimes tempting to spend the time talking together and counseling one another. But when we get right down to praying, those times have been the richest. We have found that our minds are focused and able to pray with great fervency and courage when we follow such a pattern.

The result has been remarkable. Nothing short of amazing. Week after week we have seen God change our hearts. We have seen God work in our families. We have witnessed specific and direct answers to prayer. We have been encouraged even in God's answers regarding our nation and its leaders.

You can imagine how this time of prayer then spills over into our personal, daily lives. It has a way of putting our thoughts right and causing us to think about God throughout the day.

If you don't have such a group, talk to God about it. Perhaps He has a friend or group of friends He can bring alongside you as you pray. Communal prayer will go miles in shaping your own secret time with the Lord.

By the way, let me ask you another question. How can you teach your children to pray? The obvious answer is by praying with them. In his book *The Soul-Winner,* Spurgeon writes:

> It is a very excellent method, I think, actually to take the children one by one into your room alone, and pray with them. You will see your children converted when God gives you to individualize their cases, to agonize for them, and to take them one by one, and with the door closed, to pray both with them and for them.[47]

Fathers and mothers, crawl under the covers at night, hold your little ones in your arms, and pray for them. They will never forget it. And when they grow older, pause with them before they walk out the door on their way to class. Pray with them regarding their upcoming day. Even the most rebellious children like to know that their parents pray for them.

Concentrated Private Prayer

The second form of prayer is focused private prayer in your place of personal sanctuary. And it is this form of prayer that we are most concerned with in this chapter. "Of all things," said William Wilberforce, "guard against neglecting God in the secret place of prayer." Jesus commanded us to enter into our room and pray in secret, "and your Father who sees what is done in secret will reward you" (Matthew 6:6). Private prayer is commanded by God.

But mark my words. The discipline of private prayer is probably the most difficult known to man. Don't become discouraged when you find yourself struggling to build it into your life. Adam Clarke said, "Prayer requires more of the heart than of the tongue." And in our hearts we fight our greatest battles when it comes to prayer.

Private prayer is hard for many reasons.

In Private Prayer We Encounter Resistance

Satan doesn't want us to pray. And our sinful nature fights praying. You can talk to your spouse, your friends, and your co-workers. You can talk on the phone for hours. And in all those conversations, you will probably experience very little resistance. You can e-mail everyone in the known world without encountering a great deal of distress. But try talking to God and the resistance is unbelievable. When we go to pray, we have to get over that hurdle.

One of our sons got into bodybuilding. It was a surprise to us because the year before he had trashed his body with fast food, donuts, and Coke. But then he discovered something. When he ate right and worked out, he felt a hundred times better. When he first started his workouts, he would sometimes say, "Gee, I really don't want to go do this!" But when he came home, he was invigorated! As a result, he began to get in shape and experience the rewards of his efforts. Overcoming the natural lethargy and resistance was hard at first. But gradually he came to love working out.

It's the same with prayer. The initial pattern is hard to develop, but once prayer becomes part of your life you become dependent on it—and look forward to it with great anticipation.

In Private Prayer We Find It Hard to Concentrate

In private prayer we have to switch gears mentally—from thinking about life as we see it, to thinking about life as God sees it. That doesn't just happen. It takes effort. It involves putting aside our daily, worldly thoughts and taking on heavenly, biblical thoughts. It requires entering mentally into His presence, even though we do not visually see Him. Talking with God requires looking into the Scriptures, for that is where we will see His handiwork and hear His voice. And it requires visualizing Him as He is described in Scripture, in such passages as Isaiah 6 or Daniel 10 or Revelation 1.

Because our modern minds tend to wander when they are not stimulated by sound or entertainment, we have to develop a taste for quiet and a skill for waiting before Him in His presence. That's why I have personally found it helpful to keep a pen and notebook handy. Somehow, writing down prayers helps me to focus. And it gives me the added benefit of looking back at what God has been doing in my life. It also helps me to keep another small pad to the side, on which I can write distracting thoughts to myself, like "to do" lists that pop into my mind, drive me crazy, and threaten to pull me off course. If I can just write these things down, I can get back to the business at hand.

I also like to pray on long walks. Somehow, being outside frees my mind and encourages me to look upward and talk to God. When I am walking, I release the daily pressures and "get it all out." Only the Lord knows how many times those walks have changed the course of my life, and the lives of those for whom I often pray.

When I can't walk, for one reason or another, I like to go to a restaurant and find an isolated spot where I can read and pray. I've almost worn out one McDonald's bench near my home!

The bottom line is this. Find a way to focus in on God. This work of drawing near to God is a work rewarded.

"Draw near to God and He will draw near to you" (James 4:8).

In Private Prayer We Feel That We Are Being Unproductive

Private prayer can seem hard because we often feel that we are accomplishing so little. It can seem far easier to go out and "make things happen" than to pray and ask God to handle things instead. Prayer seems so "unproductive," so "passive." Perhaps this is why prayer is often a last resort for us, *after* we have done everything we can possibly think of for a given situation.

Yet God wants us to pray *before* we act. This sounds like a revolutionary concept and goes against the natural mind, but understand an important point here. *We are not saying that we are not to act.* We are saying, instead, that our actions should be bathed in prayer *before* we undertake them.

Things happen when we pray first. Oftentimes we experience a change of mind and heart. At other times we realize that it's better not to act at all. God sometimes goes ahead of us and works things out *before* we can act. Either way, prayer brings a certain healthy restraint into our otherwise undisciplined lives. It develops a certain dependence on God in whatever we are doing, and this is what He wants.

Odd as it might seem, there is no activity *more* productive than prayer. "None can believe how powerful prayer is, and what it is able to effect, but those who have learned it by experience," said Martin Luther.

How, then, do you build a daily habit of private prayer? You set a simple plan and then *do it*. How you do it is really up to you. You set the time, you set the pattern, you set the place. And then get after it. Pursue. Refuse to turn back or become discouraged. Our Lord wants us to "always pray and not give up" (Luke 18:1, NIV).

You might begin with five or ten minutes. You talk to God and then open up the Bible and do a little reading. Or if you prefer to start with the Scriptures, you might read a psalm or the Lord's Prayer and see where that leads you.

Most important, don't give up if you struggle in the beginning. And don't lose heart if you're sometimes blown off course. Many who learn to be real prayer warriors have difficulty getting started. In time, you too will discover the approach that will work best for you, given your personality and the demands on your time. And you will come to love and cherish those quiet moments of talking with God.

As you begin, keep a few things in mind:

- *Try praying from Scripture,* for then your thoughts will be centered on God's thoughts and promises.
- *Pray in your sanctuary,* for then you can quiet your spirit to enter into His presence and focus on Him.
- *Begin and end with thanksgiving and worship of God.* There is no better way to establish a sense of faith and hope in your prayers. And you will find no better example of such praying than in the Psalms.
- *Pray honestly.* God knows your heart. He isn't freaked out by what He sees there. He loves you, and He looks for those who are honest before Him.

> Let us draw near with a sincere heart in
> full assurance of faith. (Hebrews 10:22)

- *Pray specifically.* Make your specific requests known to Him; this is His command.

> Let your requests be made known to
> God. (Philippians 4:6)

- *Pray persistently.* If your heart has a particular burden, *don't give up.* Winston Churchill is known for the famous speech in which he said, "Never, never, never give up!" Churchill could have been speaking to us. Give the Lord time to accomplish His good purposes. He hears your prayer, and His timing is always best.
- *Pray believing.*

> He who comes to God must believe
> that He is and that He is a rewarder of
> those who seek Him. (Hebrews 11:6)

There is tremendous freedom in talking with God. Some people sing. Some people write. Some people talk out loud. Sometimes your heart will be cold; you can express that to Him. Other times you will be burdened beyond words; your tears alone will speak volumes.

However you choose to pray, remember this. God delights in your prayers. He hears your prayers. He answers your prayers.

Continual Prayer

The third form of prayer is continual prayer. It means praying to God as you walk through your day.

Most Christians practice this kind of prayer in some way. And so do many non-Christians, as a matter of fact. But the best kind of continual prayer is the kind that grows out of concentrated private prayer. If you have not taken time for private prayer, however, don't let that keep you from praying throughout your day! The Lord hears our prayers wherever we are and no matter what we are doing.

The apostle Paul urges us to "pray without ceasing" (1 Thessalonians 5:17). But how in the world do we do that? The answer lies in a continual *attitude* of walking with God. Walter Mueller said: "Prayer is not merely an occasional impulse to which we respond when we are in trouble; prayer is a life attitude." Continual prayer should become part of the warp and woof of your life

- *when you awaken and when you fall to sleep.*

> The Puritans called prayer the "key of the morning and the lock of the night." And the psalmist said: "Evening and morning and at noon I will pray" (Psalm 55:17, NKJV). When you open your eyes in the morning, you greet the Lord. When you close them to sleep at night, you thank Him for another day.

- *as you go about living your life.*

When you're changing diapers, making presentations at work, disciplining your children, meeting clients, or grocery shopping. God desires that we do so in an attitude of prayer.

Does this mean that you don't fully focus on your work? No, it just means that even in your work, you are practicing the presence of God. You are working as unto Him, first and foremost.

The brilliant writer G. K. Chesterton said: "You say grace before meals. All right. But I say grace before the concert and the opera, and grace before the play and pantomime, and grace before I open a book, and grace before sketching, painting, swimming, fencing, boxing, walking, playing, dancing, and grace before I dip the pen in ink."

Continual prayer means that you are working in His presence—or *coram deo*, which translates as "living in the presence of God." And it means that you are talking with Him in the idle moments—when temptation beckons you to look with lust at another woman, when you are feeling anxious about the next event of your day, when you are beginning a conversation, when you are convicted of prideful thinking and confess it in your heart.

Such continual prayer is life changing. It's hard to lie to a client when you are working in His presence. It's tough to scream at your children when you are aware that the Lord is right there. And it's impossible to look at pornography and pray simultaneously. No wonder Paul said to "pray without ceasing"!

Crisis Praying

There is one last additional kind of prayer. It is very real. Crisis praying is a special kind of impassioned prayer in moments of great crisis and pain—when the overload in your life is about to smash you like a bug on the sidewalk.

Crisis praying is when you pull out all the stops. You stop whatever you're doing and pray fervently. You seek His face regarding some deep crisis or a huge decision in your life. You call friends around the country and ask them to pray. You get your wife, and perhaps your kids, and you pray earnestly as a family. You fast for a period of time, if God so leads you. You plead before God, holding forth His promises from Scripture.

In such times, we are utterly needy and dependent.

In such times, we will not *survive* unless the Lord comes through for us.

In such a time, Aaron and Hur held up the hands of Moses during the battle against the Amalekites (Exodus 17). And God moved mightily on their behalf.

In such a time, Elijah called out to God before the prophets of Baal. And God answered miraculously.

In such a time, Abraham Lincoln fell on his knees in his White House bedroom. He once said: "I have been driven many times to my knees by the overwhelming conviction that I had nowhere else to go. My own wisdom and that of all about me seemed insufficient for the day."

In such a time, Jesus prayed in the Garden of Gethsemane. He was in the deepest crisis of His life, and He needed His Father to see Him through.

When crisis comes our way, the promises of God become our bread. And praying those promises becomes our depressurizing chamber. "Pleading the promises of God is the whole secret of prayer, I sometimes think," said D. Martyn Lloyd-Jones.

Sometimes God purposefully allows all the props to be knocked out from under us so He can demonstrate to us that He answers prayer. And when God comes through in the clutch, we have a memorial stone to go back to time and again.

Mary and I have such memorial stones. Let me tell you about just one!

A LESSON IN LITTLE ROCK

Thirteen years ago we were getting ready for a new chapter in our lives, involving a change in ministry—and a change in location, too. We had been in Little Rock, Arkansas, for four years and were moving to Dallas.

But it was a terrible time to put a house on the market in Little Rock. We put out our sign in February, hoping to sell and move into a new home in Dallas in time for our kids to start school in August.

In two months we had exactly one showing. Things were not looking good. During this entire time we prayed earnestly, asking God to make a way for us. But our house, along with many others, languished on the market. The buyers just weren't out there.

A friend of mine mentioned to me that there were very few four-bedroom houses for rent in our area. I followed up and found that there weren't *any* available—but the demand was high. So we decided to try something a little out of our comfort zone. We put an ad in the paper to rent our home— and I tacked on the possibility of a lease with an option to buy.

The ad came out on Saturday morning and by Saturday night we had it rented, to a very sharp couple who indicated they might be interested in buying the place within the next six months. We were ecstatic. Now we could make our plans for Dallas. But two hours later they called and said they had changed their minds. What an incredible disappointment!

That night I had trouble sleeping. For two hours everything had been worked out, and then we were right back in the same boat. Our hopes had been dashed. We prayed together that night and asked God to make it possible for us to make our move. But time was getting short.

The next afternoon, Mary took the kids down to the neighborhood pool. I had received a call from another couple who wanted to see the house. They wanted to come right over and I said that would be fine.

The doorbell rang and there stood an all-American family—a father, mother, and four stairstep kids. They looked all over the house as I watched a golf tournament downstairs. About ten minutes later, the husband came down.

"I saw your books upstairs. Are you a Christian?" He asked.

I said that I was.

"Well, my wife loves your house. I'm finishing my medical residency, and I'm joining a practice here in town. We've been praying about finding just the right place for our family. I'd like to lease your house for a year, then I would be in a position to come up with a down payment. But I just don't have the money to buy it right now."

"That's no problem. I'm sure we can work something out."

We talked for another half hour and agreed to meet the

next day to sign the lease. We prayed together before they left. I don't know who was more excited. What a great answer to prayer!

About fifteen minutes later they called back and asked if they could bring their pastor by to see the house. "Sure, come on over," I said.

They came back, showed the pastor everything, and then we all prayed together. They left, and once again we were all excited.

About forty-five minutes later they called again. The husband asked if his spouse could bring the pastor's wife over to see the house. She had just got home, had heard the news, and was all excited. "Sure, bring her over."

So here they came again. Once more they walked through the house. It turns out they were best friends with the pastor and his wife. By that time we were all old friends, having a great time. We prayed together once more before they piled into their car and took off.

Five minutes later, Mary walked in with the kids. I told her all that had happened in the three hours while she'd been at the pool. She couldn't believe it. What an answer to prayer! We could go ahead and move to Dallas. The house was leased for the next twelve months, and then they would buy it. We couldn't believe how the Lord had worked things out...except that He wasn't quite through yet.

The next day we went to lunch at Chili's to celebrate and

make plans to go to Dallas later in the week to look for a new place. As I walked to our table, a guy that I barely knew said hi as we went by. He attended another church, and we had some mutual friends. He told me he'd heard through the grapevine that we were moving to Dallas. And then he said, "Have you sold your house yet?"

"Well, as a matter of fact, I just leased it to a young doctor who's joining a practice here in town. He's hoping to buy it next year—when he can get the money together for a down payment."

"You're kidding," he said. "May I ask who this young doctor is?"

I told him the name and he said, "I know Scott. In fact, he's joining *my* practice."

I laughed and said, "What a small world! You ought to give him a raise so he can buy my house."

We all chuckled.

The next night I got a call from Scott.

"Steve, you're not going to believe this, but I've got the down payment! We can go ahead and buy your house now!"

I was shocked. "That's incredible, Scott. How in the world did you do it?"

"Well, after you ran into Tom at Chili's yesterday and told him we were going to lease the house, he gave me a call. He asked me if my wife really liked your house enough to eventually buy it. I told him she loved it—she loved everything about it. He said, 'Well, why don't we just go ahead and advance you money to buy it?'"

Just three nights before, I had been so upset because the first couple had backed out on renting our house. I couldn't understand why God wasn't answering our prayers. But He *was!* We just didn't understand because we were still in the middle of it.

We had been waiting for months to sell that house. We were tired of waiting on God, and we were tired of praying. Little did we know, in our Saturday evening of disappointment, that we were just three days away from an amazing answer.

So what are you waiting on God to do?

Chapter Six

AFFLUENZA:
You Need to Simplify

"Every increased possession loads us with a new weariness."

JOHN RUSKIN

A few years ago, my grandmother died at the age of 101. She had twelve brothers and sisters. When they'd all reached adulthood, the kids held a family reunion every year. As time went by, that reunion began to include children, grandchildren, and even great-grandchildren. More than three hundred people often showed up.

But Nana's two oldest brothers never came. And it was always a great sadness when their names were brought up. Everyone missed Troy and Harry. They both died as young men in 1918.

Now a lot of young men died that year in World War I, but that's not what took the lives of Troy and Dallas. Those two young men, in the prime of their lives, died from the flu. That's a hard thing to imagine in this day and age, but they were not alone. In 1918, more than 500,000 Americans died of the same disease.

The 1918 influenza epidemic was the most destructive in history. In fact, it ranks with the plague of Justinian and the black death as one of the most severe holocausts of disease ever visited upon the earth. It was estimated "that more than 20 million persons perished of influenza in a few months and more than 50 times as many were sick. In the United States, 548,000 died. In India, 12,500,000 persons, or 4% of the total population, [were] said to have been killed by influenza in the autumn of 1918."[48]

Can you imagine 20 million people dying from the flu? However, as incredible as that seems, another epidemic was even more devastating. Between 1347 and 1370, nearly 40 million died from the black death, or the plague. Estimates vary, but this deadly epidemic wiped out somewhere between one-third and one-half of the entire population of Europe.

Precisely what was the black death? Plague is primarily a disease common to rodents, especially rats. The rat flea carries it from one rat to another, but human beings can catch it if they become infested with fleas. In the crowded conditions of medieval cities, whole populations commonly did just that. In times of extreme stress, during sieges or famines, city dwellers were especially at risk. If plague became epidemic, as often happened, the death toll soared because there was no known cure and no knowledge of what caused it in the first place. Only modern sanitation can prevent it, and only modern antibiotics can control it.

A MODERN EPIDEMIC

I don't know any families who have lost a child to influenza. And I don't currently know of any families in our neighborhood who are desperately trying to fight off the plague. Medical research and technology now routinely protect us against horrific diseases that once wiped out entire families, neighborhoods, and even cities.

But another epidemic is now taking a tremendous toll on our children. It is not influenza and it is not the plague. I call it *affluenza.*

It doesn't come from rats. It comes from the rat race.

Now I lay me down to sleep
I pray my Cuisinart to keep
I pray my stocks are on the rise
And that my analyst is wise
That all the wine I sip is white
And that my hot tub's watertight
That racquetball won't get too tough
That all my sushi's fresh enough
I pray my cell-phone battery works

That my career won't lose its perks
My microwave won't radiate
My condo won't depreciate
I pray my health club doesn't close
And that my money market grows
If I go broke before I wake
I pray my Volvo they won't take.[49]

Affluenza is not restricted to wealthy families. It's becoming increasingly more epidemic in the "lives of those who are merely well-off, who are comfortably middle-class, or who simply aspire to greater incomes, acquisitions and status."[50] In other words, the majority of families in America are now at risk.

Affluenza attacks relationships. Family relationships. And our children suffer the most. Affluenza causes parents to lose their minds and sacrifice their children on the altar of success.

But affluenza almost never reveals itself in the clear light of day. It's a subtle killer, a spiritual virus that creeps up on people before they realize they've been afflicted. Affluenza manifests itself in:

1. a reaching for more and more, in spite of what we already have,
2. an insatiable drive to be successful,

3. a chronic lack of contentment,
4. a consistent choosing of career over family relationships,
5. an overscheduled, overloaded life that leaves no room for significant time with spouse and children.

PRESSURE COOKER FAMILIES

A family afflicted with affluenza is characterized by pressure and busyness. Their schedules become so full they have no downtime, no family time, no time to eat a meal together, no time to enjoy a meaningful conversation. They leave themselves no time to discover what's going on inside their children's heads, no time to work through conflict, no time to think and plan together about the kind of life they really want to live.

And there is fear. Fear that if we slow or stop this pace, we will somehow "miss out" and our children will be left behind in the dust. This fear generates a tremendous pressure to succeed, pressure to keep up. And that's followed, of course, by pressure to stay on top, pressure to be number one, pressure to excel in career, athletics, and school.

Affluenza causes parents

- to give their children too much freedom and too little attention,
- to give their kids too many things and too little time,

- to pressure their children to perform rather than encouraging them to develop natural skills at a natural pace,
- to give their children too much information, which erodes their moral innocence,
- to focus on acquiring an image rather than achieving character.

YOU NEED SIMPLICITY

So what's the cure? Well, affluenza is both complex and deceptive. The more you have, the more energy you spend to maintain what you don't need. But the cure is just the opposite; it's called *simplicity.*

Randy Alcorn tells the story of a man who ran into a friend at the airport. The man looked very troubled.

"What's the matter?" Hugh asked.

The man sighed. "I thought I was finally going to have a weekend to myself. But now I have to go supervise repairs on my house in Florida." Dejected, he sat waiting to take off in his private jet.

Here's a man with everything he needs, with what most people dream of; yet he couldn't even enjoy his weekend. He was enslaved by his possessions. We think we own our possessions, but too often they own us."51

This man would be better off if he simplified his life.

So how do we simplify? The cure has five parts. To defeat affluenza,

1. you need *contentment,*
2. you need a *compass,*
3. you need to *cut it out,*
4. you need to *conserve,*
5. you need to *cultivate.*

It doesn't get much simpler than that.

YOU NEED CONTENTMENT

I was fine until I picked up the magazine. In fact, I was doing great. I was tired, because I had just spend six hours mowing our yard on a sweltering, smothering summer day. The temperature hovered close to one hundred degrees, and the humidity registered more than 90 percent. As I sat down to guzzle my iced tea, I had a real feeling of accomplishment. The yard looked like a million bucks and so did our ten-year-old house with its new coat of paint.

As I said, I was fine until I picked up that magazine. After several minutes of cooling down and sipping tea, I started flipping through the pages. I stopped to notice the pictures in an article that profiled a couple in Des Moines. They had just remodeled their eleven-year-old kitchen, and the finished product looked incredible.

I flipped a few more pages and noticed a do-it-yourself feature on putting a deck in your backyard. I already had one, but to tell you the truth, it didn't look anything like the deck in the magazine. Until then I'd been perfectly happy; in fact, I had spent a great deal of time that very afternoon sitting on that deck as I took breaks from the blasting heat. I'd had a real sense of contentment and enjoyment on that deck, as I sat drinking my iced tea under our thirty-foot maple tree. Come to think of it, I was fine until I picked up that magazine.

Do you see the remarkable transformation that took place? Just five or six minutes earlier, I had sat down with a real sense of contentment. I was proud of my home and how it looked.

And yet, within minutes I could hardly stomach the idea of living in such a roach trap. Look at the kitchen! Those countertops are Formica! We need to get some countertops with ceramic tile—this place looks like something Roy Rogers might use to serve his buckaroos on a cattle drive. Military personnel in Afghanistan are eating in canvas mess halls that look better than this dump!

And look at these cabinets. I've seen firewood in better shape. The magazine showed a pantry that opened up to reveal multiple shelves that rotated in a circle, at the touch of a button. Look at this dump we call a pantry. It's about as well organized as the backpack of a five-year-old on his way to kindergarten. We have cans of soup in there somewhere that are three or four years old. At least I think we do. We put things in our pantry and never see them again. If we could get to all that stuff, we could feed a small country for a month! What we need are some rotating, motorized cabinets around here!

How did I go so quickly from satisfaction to disgust? The answer is "comparison." I was perfectly happy until I began leafing through the glossy pages of that magazine… and began making comparisons.

By the way, the magazine I was reading circulates to 7.6 million readers. It's known as *Homes and Gardens.* No, that's not quite right. It's *BETTER Homes and Gardens.* Better than whose? Better than mine!

No wonder America is so driven. Think of it. Every month, eight million people are reminded that someone out there has something that's better than what they have. It might be a deck, a house, or a garden…but it's *better than theirs!*

I have a question for you.

What would it take to make you happy?

- A remodeled kitchen?
- A bigger house?
- A new SUV?

For others it may be a romantic husband, a serving wife, or a child who is compliant in nature and successful in school.

In Philippians 4:11–12, the apostle Paul writes:

> For I have learned to be content in whatever circumstances I am. I know how to get along with humble means, and I also know how to live in prosperity; in any and every circumstance I have learned the secret of being filled and going hungry, both of having abundance and suffering need.

When Paul wrote these words, he was in prison. Prison does not represent the best of circumstances. But Paul had learned to be content and joyful, no matter where the Lord led him.

Contentment must be learned. It doesn't come naturally to us; we tend to concentrate on how things could be better. That's where comparison slips in the back door and robs us of contentment.

Comparison is the enemy of contentment. We must learn to be content in the will and the goodness of God, even when things could be better...because they *always* could be as long as we're still on Earth!

Paul could be content in a five-star hotel...or in prison.

Paul could be content driving a new BMW...or a '64 Volkswagen.

Paul had learned that he didn't need *more* to be content, nor did he need a different set of circumstances. That was his secret. He could be content right where he was. And he did this through the life-changing power of Christ.

As he spoke about contentment, his very next words were: "I can do all things through Him who strengthens me" (Philippians 4:13).

Contentment is a wonderful thing. Contentment brings happiness and satisfaction. It also carries with it a thankful spirit and a perspective of gratitude. By contrast, we tend to *compare* ourselves with people who have more than we do. Why not compare yourself to people who have less?

If you're bothered that you don't have a nicer bathroom, why don't you compare yourself to someone who doesn't have indoor plumbing at all?

If you're unhappy because you really need a bigger house for your growing family, then why not compare yourself to the impoverished family who sleeps ten to a room? That kind of comparison will make you thankful and content in a hurry.

The first step toward contentment is thankfulness. And thankfulness is an attitude, an approach to life. Thankfulness leads to contentment and overcoming overload.

Do you recall what we said earlier, that children pick up affluenza from their parents? Kids also pick up on the reverse, real fast, if their parents are content and happy.

Tonight at dinner, why don't you do something different when you pray? As your family bows and you lead them in prayer, thank God that you have water—*clean* water. Thank the Lord that you have food to eat that is *not* infested with worms or flies. Thank God for your electricity. Thank Him for your indoor bathrooms. And thank Him that your children will have hot water for their baths before bed.

I think you get the idea.

That kind of prayer will bring contentment to your family in a big hurry. And it will put a stop to the petty whining so characteristic of affluenza.

YOU NEED A COMPASS

In this world of materialism and pressure to succeed, it's easy to get lost. That's why you need a compass. A compass provides perspective and tells you which way you are going. It's calibrated to what is known as "true north."

Another kind of compass will keep you off the path to affluenza. Matthew 6:33 says: "But seek *first* His kingdom and His righteousness, and all these things will be added to you."

Seeking the kingdom of God *first* will calibrate your life and keep you pointed away from the false path of affluenza. The psalmist wrote: "Direct me in the path of your commands, for there I find delight.... Because I consider all your precepts right, I hate every wrong path" (Psalm 119:35, 128, NIV).

Don't seek success first—seek Christ.

Don't seek prominence and promotion first—seek integrity and righteousness and the approval of Christ in your work.

So what's first in your life? What are you pursuing like a heat-seeking missile? It is knowing Christ and being a godly man or woman? Or is it something else? Any pursuit other than seeking Him first is ultimately cheap and worthless. Don't seek the world's agenda first.

Seek God's agenda.

Seek God's plan.

Seek God's blueprint.

Seek these things with all your heart, soul, mind, and strength.

If you are seeking Christ first, following His blueprint for marriage will be a priority for you—and divorce will not be an option.

If you are putting Christ first, you will communicate with your spouse and work out your conflicts and differences to the glory of God.

If your are seeking Christ first, you will follow His guidelines for raising your children instead of the world's system.

I have covered this extensively in my book *Gettin' There,*

so I will just touch on it here. Every family at its core needs two things: provision and care. Provision is food, shelter, and clothing. Care is love, affection, nourishment, and emotional security. Do you know any family that does *not* need those two things?

In Scripture, God has appointed the man as the primary provider. He has appointed the wife as the primary caregiver. Yet our culture says that both husbands and wives should be working full-time to make provision. So...who is caring for the children? You must answer that question before the Lord.

So many good families have convinced themselves that they must have two incomes to get by. But that simply is not true. And believing that lie may cost you more than your realize. Andy Dappen gives some free advice on the subject:

> My wife and I used to think that we needed two incomes.... We were wrong.
>
> After our two children were born, my wife began working part-time as a teacher, earning less than $30,000 a year. That $30,000 boiled down to $10,000 in disposable income after all work-related expenses, child care, and taxes came out.
>
> But we found out that we could save that same $10,000 a year by reducing expenses, if she made the

home and family a full-time job. And we'd be taking care of our family in the process.[52]

What kind of balance is in your home when it comes to provision and care? Are you top-heavy on provision and low on care? Why not ask God to help you find the balance that your children need? Wouldn't it make a huge difference if both of you didn't work full-time? It would lower the stress and the pace of your life. And yes, it might lower your income! But maybe it wouldn't lower it as much as you think.

YOU NEED TO CUT IT OUT

Is your life cluttered with nonstop commitments and clutter?

You need to cut it out!

You need to have a garage sale and get rid of that stuff.

What I have in mind here is not the garage attached to your house. I'm talking about unloading your schedule and your commitments.

Just last weekend I spoke with a man who told me he'd been dealing with overload for the last year. He owns his own company and averages sixty to seventy hours a week at work. I asked him what he did in his spare time. He told me that he served on the boards of twenty-two separate ministries. No wonder he's overloaded. He needs to clean out the garage.

Cleaning out the garage of your life is a matter of priorities. It's a matter of saying no to very *good* things so you can say yes to *better* things. What goes and what stays? You might get your spouse or a good friend to help you decide. It's always easier to clean out the garage when you have help. Sit down and show them your schedule. Explain your priorities. And let them help you sort out the junk in your life. When you have a friend to help you, cleaning out the garage is not an overwhelming task.

I have traveled in a conference ministry since 1990. Most weekends I'm far from home, speaking somewhere across the United States. I love it and am privileged to do it. But last year I noticed something for the first time. The traveling was starting to get to me.

Mary and I sat down and looked at my schedule. Two things became very obvious. I needed to step back from one of the Bible studies I was teaching in Dallas during the week. I could handle one, but not two.

Then I had a conversation with my friend, Gary Rosberg. Gary does what I do, so he intimately understood my situation. Following that conversation I made two more changes. First, I decided not to stay over after a conference and speak on Sunday. Our conferences would run Friday evening and all day Saturday. Usually I would speak six to seven times. More often than not, the host church would then ask me to speak in their services on Sunday. That could equal two and sometimes three services in addition to the seven I had already committed to.

So Gary, Mary, and I came up with a policy. When I'm invited to stay over and speak on Sunday, the answer is no. It's a polite no, but it's definite. That move right there gave me twenty-five more days a year to be in church with my own family on Sunday.

Second, we began concluding our conferences at noon on Saturday instead of going to 4 P.M. And that gave me four extra hours of travel time so I could get back home by Sunday morning.

Those were the best two moves I've made in a long time! Believe me, there's nothing like a clean garage.

YOU NEED TO CONSERVE

Recently I walked into a store in California that had a big sign posted on several different walls.

WE ARE CONSERVING ENERGY. WE HAVE TURNED OUT ONE-THIRD OF OUR LIGHTS TO SAVE ENERGY AND CUT COSTS!

Quite frankly, there was plenty of light in that store. If I hadn't seen the sign I never would have known that they were cutting back. But they were. And it was a very wise move.

G. K. Chesterton once said, "There are two ways to get enough. One is to accumulate more and more. The other is to desire less."

We can all find areas where we can cut our expenses. Many people have had to significantly cut their expenses over the last year or so because of the drop in the stock market. Money is not flowing as freely as it did in the '90s. So businesses are cutting expenses and so are families.

In the last two years we have gone through a process of downsizing our ministry in order to be more effective. We changed the way we were structuring our conferences. We weren't sure how these changes would actually work out, but God worked everything out! As a result, we have reduced our staffing and costs by approximately 70 percent. Yet we are ministering to just as many people as before.

You've heard the adage, "Less is more."

That is a true statement. It's true for a ministry or business, and it's true for a family. Spending less is a simple way to simplify your life.

YOU NEED TO CULTIVATE

I have a friend who's a farmer in Nebraska. Ron cultivates more than three thousand acres. His family depends on good crops of corn, wheat, and soybeans each year.

But if Ron doesn't plant, Ron doesn't reap. That's pretty

basic, isn't it? In fact, nothing could be more obvious. If you don't plant, you won't get a harvest. The same is true in the Christian life.

Cultivation, in the Christian life, is called *giving*. And giving is another antidote to the virus of affluenza. Let me introduce you to a small but wonderful book by my friend Randy Alcorn. It's called *The Treasure Principle.* This little book is only ninety-two pages long, but as far as I'm concerned, it's a must-read. It contains an explosive message that will "free you up" in many ways.

In this short chapter I can give you only a small taste of the biblical concepts that Randy lays out so well. But perhaps a taste will provoke a desire to begin the process in your own life.

Let's start with a simple admission. Many of you who are reading this aren't giving at all. That is a major mistake. George Barna has done some research on the giving habits of born-again Christians:

Among born again adults, there was a 44 percent rise in those who gave nothing last year. Compared to 1999, the mean per capita donation to churches dropped by 19 percent in 2000. One-third of born again adults said they tithed in 2000, but a comparison of their actual giving and household incomes reveals that only one-eighth did so.[53]

In the Old Testament, God's people once began failing to give as they should. God spoke to them through the prophet Malachi:

"Will a man rob God? Yet you rob me. But you ask, 'How do we rob you?' In tithes and offerings. You are under a curse—the whole nation of you—because you are robbing me. Bring the whole tithe into the storehouse, that there may be food in my house" (Malachi 3:8–10, NIV).

The "tithe" was a tenth part of their income. Ten percent was to be returned to the Lord. And Proverbs 3:9 states, "Honor the LORD from your wealth and from the first of all your produce."

Here's how the Lord meant for this to work. When the harvest first came in, they were to give to God first. That was a scary thing! If you gave to the Lord from the first of the wheat, what if a fire came and burned the rest of the crop? You would be financially ruined, but you would also have nothing to feed your children.

God wanted his people to give to Him first, *trusting* that He would meet whatever needs developed later. Giving first to God is an act of trust and an expression of faith in His character. But the tithe was the standard that God had set:

"A tithe of everything from the land, whether grain from the soil or fruit from the trees, belongs to the LORD; it is holy to the LORD" (Leviticus 27:30, NIV).

So does the concept of a tithe still apply to us today? I

like the balance and wisdom that Randy Alcorn brings to that question:

> Jesus validated the mandatory tithe, even on small things (Matthew 23:23). But there's no mention of tithing after the Gospels. It's neither commanded nor rescinded, and there's heated debate among Christians about whether tithing is still a starting place for giving.
>
> I have mixed feelings on this issue. I detest legalism. I certainly don't want to try to pour new wine into old wineskins, imposing superseded First Covenant restrictions on Christians. Every New Testament example of giving goes far beyond the tithe. However, none falls short of it.
>
> There's a timeless truth behind the concept of giving God our firstfruits. Whether or not the tithe is still the minimal measure of those firstfruits, I ask myself, *Does God expect His New Covenant children to give less or more?* Jesus raised the spiritual bar; He never lowered it (Matthew 5:27–28).[54]

But we can't *afford* to give!

That's always our first response. Especially when we find ourselves in a tight financial situation. I will never forget something that happened years ago.

My mom and dad had experienced a major setback financially. They had made a major investment that had gone under. My parents had always tithed, but things were so tight they decided they just couldn't do it. So they didn't. And things didn't improve. This went on for months. And then it went on for more months.

Finally, my dad became convicted. He became convinced that his lack of faith was a major cause of their financial difficulty. And my mother agreed, so they began tithing again. This was a tremendous step of faith for them because the money just wasn't there. But they purposed in their heart to give a tenth back to God, of whatever came in.

That year their income doubled from the previous year.

Not too long after that, they decided that they should increase their giving. So, instead of giving 10 percent, they upped it to 20 percent. That next year their income increased ten times. They actually gave more that year in tithes than they had made the previous year. Did you catch that? Their income had increased so much that their tithe was larger than their total income for the previous year!

My dad and mom decided to tithe when they couldn't afford it. They gave to the Lord *first* and trusted Him to provide their mortgage payment. And He did. In fact, God didn't just provide. He opened the windows of heaven.

But that is what He promised to do through the prophet

Malachi. Earlier we quoted the Scripture from Malachi—
but we only cited half of it. Here's the rest of the story:

> "Will a man rob God? Yet you rob me. But you ask,
> 'How do we rob you?' In tithes and offerings. You are
> under a curse—the whole nation of you—because
> you are robbing me. Bring the whole tithe into the
> storehouse, that there may be food in my house. Test
> me in this," says the LORD Almighty, "and see if I will
> not throw open the floodgates of heaven and pour
> out so much blessing that you will not have room
> enough for it." (Malachi 3:8–10, NIV)

A number of years ago, Pepsi created an ad campaign
featuring something called "the Pepsi challenge." The soft
drink giant asked consumers to compare their brand of fizz
with that of their rival. This is the tithing challenge. And
God is the One who challenges you to test Him. You think
you can't afford to test Him? You can't afford *not* to test
Him!

When my dad's accountant found out he was tithing, the
guy went nuts! And he was a Christian. He told my dad that
he was in no position to tithe.

The fact is, we are *always* in a position to tithe. We are
always in a position to trust the living God to meet our
needs.

The accountant told my dad that he needed to invest that money instead of tithing it. Well, my dad did invest it. What investment do you know of that gives a tenfold yield? There were a few dot-coms whose stock did pretty well for a while. But what is that stock worth now? And what will it be worth in eternity?

I was a college kid when my parents went through that difficult time. Quite frankly, I didn't learn a whole lot in college. But I got a real education watching my parents trust God with their tithe. Why don't you do that for your kids? Do what you think you can't afford to do. And then let your children see the goodness of God as He opens the windows of heaven and meets your needs.

Trusting God with your tithe will inoculate your children against affluenza. And for the rest of their lives, they will have a living example before them, proving that the promises of God can be trusted.

Summing It Up

Simplicity is a mindset that leads to some very hard choices. It is the cutting away, or trimming off, of the good in order to have the best. It is an elimination of the cholesterol that slowly but surely clogs the arteries of the soul. Simplicity is painful because it is the greatest step of trust yet. And few are those who venture to go this deep or this far. The tragedy is that if you walk away from biblical simplicity, you have really missed the very thing that overcomes overload. You've lost the very thing that changes the course of your life from that of being *momentarily* at rest to that of being *continually* at rest.

Many of the other disciplines we've discussed in the pages of this book are actions which we can implement. And we are good implementers. Simplicity, on the other hand, is a *walking away.* It is a conscious choice *not* to act, not to do. Sanctuary says yes to God. Sustenance recognizes the need for soul nourishment. Supplication understands the power of beseeching the throne of heaven. But simplicity says *no.*

No to overspending and overcommitting.

No to opportunities that tear apart families and marriages.

No to the pace.

No to the world's expectations.

And we do not like to say no. We enjoy our addictions to the pace. We love the rush of the pursuit of success. We perish at the thought of a missed opportunity or a lesser sense of accomplishment in the eyes of the world. But when we choose simplicity, we are making the hard choices that change the very core of the way we live life. Simplicity reforms our lives. Simplicity resists 24/7 at every turn and puts us on a different path, a path of clear focus and biblical living.

Ironically, most everyone I know *does* long for a simpler life. They would love to go back to the days when life was less complex. But even though we can't go back a century, every one of us can and must simplify our lives. We must work at learning how to be content. We must go back to God's blueprint and determine how He wants us to live in our marriages and with our children. The principles of marriage and parenting are His principles—and we are to conform our lives to them. We are so quick to listen to some PhD or radio talk show host, and so slow to listen to almighty God.

We must streamline our schedules and get rid of what really doesn't matter. We must cut and cut until we have made time for solitude and for those who are most important to us. Finally, we must spend less and give more, remembering at all times that it is impossible to out-give God.

A simple life is like anything of great value—it requires thought and sacrifice to achieve. But what a difference it will make in the long run! Your life could be vastly improved in just ninety days if you began today to implement these principles.

I don't know about you, but just the thought of that decreases my overload.

But let's do more than hear these truths. Let's *do* these truths. And let's do them to the glory of God.

Chapter Seven

TWO FEET OF BARK:
You Need a Sovereign

*Of all the doctrines of the Bible,
none is so offensive to human nature
as the doctrine of God's sovereignty.*

J. C. RYLE

*Oh! For a spirit that bows always
before the sovereignty of God!*

C. H. SPURGEON

L ast year we took a trip up to Sequoia National Park in the Sierra Nevada Mountains of California. Not long after that trip, a huge forest fire broke out in that area, prompting an amazing response.

Everyone was particularly concerned because of the redwoods. Now there are redwoods scattered in different places along the coast of California. But the giant redwoods, or sequoias, as they are also called, are the largest trees (by volume) in the entire world. They grow best at about five to seven thousand feet on the western slope of the Sierras. It is in this particular zone, just east of the San Joaquin Valley, where the giant redwoods have ruled and reigned for centuries.

The conditions at this elevation are absolutely perfect for these ancient ones. And they are stunning. They top out at just under three hundred feet, and the base of their trunks is over thirty-five feet in diameter. They are magnificent giants, and the sight of them up close will take your breath away.

When the fires broke out last summer, over a thousand people from "the Valley" (which is how the San Joaquin Valley is known in these parts) jumped into their cars, pickups, and SUVs and drove up to the fire lines…just to protect those trees. There had been no call from the forest service for volunteers, but when people heard the giant redwoods might be in danger, an immediate and spontaneous call to arms rang out. From all over California, people gathered what equipment they had and headed up the mountain. At all costs, those giant sequoias had to be saved. And thanks to the hundreds and hundreds of volunteers, the fire never reached those magnificent trees.

These giant sequoias truly are unbelievable masterpieces. Surprisingly, these redwood giants have root systems that go down only about four or five feet into the earth. They don't have a taproot. Although the roots are shallow, they are very expansive and wide.

There are trees in the park that are over 3,200 years old. Some of them have toppled, and there is a museum in which you can study a cross section, or crosscut of one of these massive trees—and looking at that crosscut is like reading the tree's personal history.

It quickly becomes apparent that this tree is no stranger to fire. All of the giant sequoias have been through the flames more than once. As you closely examine this cross section, you can see the actual fire marks of this tree that has endured over the centuries. It is not unusual for a tree that is 1,500 to 2,000 years old to have been through 100, 115, or 120 fires. And there were no earnest volunteers from the San Joaquin Valley coming up to protect them! So how did they survive the flames that took down all of the other trees around them?

The secret is in their bark.

The giant sequoia has a layer of bark that is two feet thick. Not three inches, eight inches, or twelve inches. But two feet! Put down this book for a moment and hold your hands two feet apart in front of you. Now do you see the

secret that keeps the sequoias alive when other trees surren-
der to the flames?

When you think about it, it really was a nice gesture on
the part of the save-the-redwoods volunteers. But these
sequoias are seasoned firefighters in their own right.

And their secret weapon is two feet of bark.

PUTTING ON THE BARK

As we were driving down the mountain after spending the
day among the giant sequoias, I realized that I needed something in my life.

I, too, need two feet of bark.

And I'm guessing you need the same thing.

We are not trees. We are people. And we need so very
much to find something that will protect us from the flames
and fires of everyday life. We are overloaded people. And
overloaded people desperately need two feet of bark—but
we have to *choose* to wrap the bark around us.

So what is this bark that will protect and defend us from
the heat and devastation raging all around us?

It is the sovereignty of God.

Previous generations of Christians found their security
and safety in the sovereignty of God. But we rarely teach or
reflect on it in our churches. No wonder we are overloaded.

So what is the sovereignty of God? What does it mean? It
is the central truth that will provide you with peace and rest

in an overloaded world. You cannot overcome overload without an understanding of this all-important truth. But for now, let's offer a very simple definition.

Sovereignty means that God is King. He rules and reigns over everyone and everything. He rules over events and circumstances. *Nothing* happens by chance.

Before the horrendous events of September 11, 2001, Todd and Lisa Beamer were not household names. But they certainly are today. We all know that Todd led a group of men to overpower the hijackers who were planning to fly United Flight 93 into the White House or the Capitol building. Because of Todd's bravery, the insane mission was aborted. He and a number of others gave their lives in a remote field in Pennsylvania to protect the lives of others in Washington, D.C.

In the aftermath, the whole nation was taken with the poise and grace of Lisa Beamer. Here was a woman who had suffered an unspeakable tragedy. Here was this young mother of two, with another on the way, fielding questions on national television about the death of her husband with such dignity and wisdom. And poise. Such poise. There was something different about Lisa Beamer—something unusual about the calm and composure in the midst of the greatest loss of her life.

Where did that come from?

Lisa Beamer believes in the sovereignty of God. That is

the secret behind her poise and composure. The sovereignty of God is her two feet of bark.

Lisa stated it this way: "My faith wasn't rooted in governments, religion, tall buildings, or frail people. My faith and my security were in God."[55]

Throughout the pages of her book, *Let's Roll,* Lisa speaks of the greatness and goodness of God. The goodness of God? How can she speak of *goodness* when God allowed her husband to be taken from her and her children? If anyone was entitled to feelings of overload, it was Lisa. She could have been overloaded with anger and self-pity, but she wasn't.

This wasn't the first time Lisa had dealt with an untimely and shocking death. When she was fifteen, her father, outwardly healthy and vigorous, was rushed to the hospital after experiencing chest pains at work. The physician who treated him that day misdiagnosed his symptoms. The doctor assured Lisa's mother that he was going to be fine, but they would keep him overnight for observation.

The next morning at five, the doctor called to say they had discovered an aortic aneurysm. Because their hospital didn't have the proper equipment for surgery, they were transporting him to another hospital. Ninety minutes later, Lisa's father died.

The man who was the rock of her existence was suddenly and unexpectedly taken away. Lisa began to have deep questions about God and His goodness. She was drawn over and over to Romans 11:33–36, a passage that speaks of the wisdom and sovereignty of God. But questions still lingered in her heart. *Why* did the doctor misdiagnose her dad's condition? *Why* wasn't he in the "right" hospital to begin with? *Why* didn't God protect her family from this terrible evil? For the next several years, she dealt with anger, bitterness, and resentment over her father's untimely death.

Lisa went on to Wheaton College and tells the story of an eventful meeting with Dennis Massaro, then director of outreach for the college. Lisa had signed up for a summer mission trip to Indonesia, and as she was discussing the trip with Dennis, the conversation turned to her bitterness over the death of her father. She was still dealing with all of the questions as to why God had taken her dad in his early fifties. All of her anger and resentment toward God came spilling out as she spoke with Dennis. Then, calmly and wisely, Dennis responded:

> "You know, Lisa, God knew the hospital they took your dad to wasn't going to have the right equipment to perform the surgery."

> I gulped hard, as though I was going to interrupt Dennis, but he paid no attention and kept right on talking.

> "The Lord knew the first doctor was going to

blow off the situation. At any time, God could have changed the circumstances. He could have changed the hospital or the doctor. Better yet, He could have healed the hole in your dad's heart. But for whatever reason, He let the natural course of things take place that day."

I blinked back the tears as Dennis continued. "Knowing what the consequences were going to be for you and your family and for you, he nonetheless allowed it to happen. Maybe it's time for you to accept that."

Dennis' gentle words were a targeted arrow in my heart. I knew he was right. And at the same time I both loved and hated him for telling me the truth. But the truth set me free.[56]

After her conversations with Dennis, she remembered the passage she had read a number of times before in her Bible. But this time when she read the words of Romans 11:33–36 (NIV), they seemed to jump off the page at her:

Oh, the depth of the riches of the wisdom and knowledge of God! How unsearchable his judgments, and his paths beyond tracing out! "Who has known the mind of the Lord? Or who has been his counselor? Who has ever given to God, that God should repay him?" For from him and through him and to him are all things. To him be the glory forever! Amen.

Lisa then recalls her reaction to this staggering description of God:

As I read those words, a thought struck me. *Who are you to question God and say that you have a better plan than He does? You don't have the same wisdom and knowledge that He has, or the understanding of the big picture. You think you deserve a happy life and get angry when it doesn't always happen like that. In fact, you are a sinner and deserve only death. The fact that God has offered you a hope for eternal life is amazing! You should be overwhelmed with joy and gratitude.*

All at once I was caught in a dichotomy: I know I'm really important to God and He truly loves me. Yet at the same time, I'm a mere mortal with limited understanding. *Who am I to question Him?* I asked myself, realizing, perhaps for the first time, how awe-inspiring God really is. It was then I made a conscious decision to stop questioning God and start trusting Him.[57]

On that day, Lisa Beamer came to grips with the sovereignty of God. On that day she began to wrap herself in two feet of bark. And by her own admission, it was this growing certainty of God's sovereignty that brought peace and rest to her heart. The overload was defeated.

Spurgeon wrote:

There is no attribute of God more comforting to His children than the doctrine of divine sovereignty. There is nothing for which the children of God ought more earnestly to contend than the Kingship of God over all the works of His own hands. On the other hand, there is no doctrine more hated by worldlings as the great, stupendous, but yet most certain doctrine of the sovereignty of the most Infinite Jehovah. Men will allow God to be everywhere except upon His throne. When God ascends His throne, His creatures gnash their teeth. When we proclaim and enthrone God and His right to do as He wills with His own, to dispose of His creatures as He thinks well, without consulting them in the matter, then it is that that makes men turn a deaf ear to us, for God on His throne is not the God they love. They love Him anywhere better than they do when He sits with His scepter in His hand and His crown upon His head. But it is God upon the throne that we love to preach. It is God upon His throne whom we trust.

What we believe about God is the most important thing about us. What Lisa learned to believe about the sovereignty of God is what sustained her through the darkest days of her life. It was the knowledge that the King of the universe was in absolute control of all things that carried her through—and comforts her to this day. She knew that this King was pure and good, and could do no wrong or evil. His character could be trusted even when circumstances did not make sense to our finite minds. The sovereignty of God was her two feet of bark. It was her protection in the greatest tragedy of her life.

So what do you believe about God? Do you share a belief with Lisa in His sovereignty? If you do, you're part of a rapidly diminishing minority.

BIBLICAL CHRISTIANS:
THE SHRINKING MINORITY

The number of Christians who believe in the sovereign God of the Bible are shrinking at a dramatic rate. How can that be? Don't all Christians believe the Bible? No, they don't. Don't all Christians who consider themselves "born again" believe the Bible? Once again, the answer is no. According to one study, the number of evangelical Christians in America has dropped from 12 percent in 1992 to just 5 percent in 2002.[58]

Someone has defined evangelical Christians as the thin

slice of people who are really biblical Christians.[59] Evangelicals hold fast to the Bible. They understand that it is the highest authority in all of life, that it is the very Word of God, just as the Bible claims. It is inerrant and infallible, and they submit their lives, hearts, and behavior to its authority.

According to Christian pollster George Barna, however, there is another group of Christians. This group he labels as "non-evangelical, born-again Christians."[60] These are people who have trusted Christ to save them from sin. But they have done so with a hitch. Barna describes these people as those who reject a key biblical doctrine.

Now, there is something here that we must clearly understand. Barna calls these people "non-evangelicals." But that is not how they refer to themselves. They believe that they *are* evangelicals, even though they don't accept the authority and teaching of the Bible. Some don't believe in hell. Some believe that God doesn't know what will happen in the future. Others reject that Jesus is the only way to God.

In other words, many of those who consider themselves evangelicals "are accepting beliefs that would have horrified [evangelical] people 50 years ago."[61] Why are they rejecting these biblical teachings? Because they have been influenced by a culture that promotes "tolerance" as the supreme virtue and that considers these teachings of the Word of God too "harsh."

They have crossed over a line. They have assumed their

own personal sovereignty over God and the Scriptures. And that is a very serious issue. In fact, it is the *core* issue.

Noah Webster defined *sovereign* as "above all others."

When we make ourselves sovereign over the Bible, to pick and choose what we like and don't like, we are placing ourselves above God. We are deciding what we consider truth rather than submitting ourselves to what God has told us is true. And that's something you don't ever want to do.

Among this group of non-evangelicals are "open theists," whose primary problem with the Bible centers on His sovereignty. Despite the teachings of Scripture, open theists have decided that God cannot be sovereign. They insist that if God is holy and loving, He cannot be in control of the world. And so they have stripped off the bark of God's sovereignty and thrown it in the dumpster. The worldly equivalent would be a park ranger peeling the two feet of bark off a giant sequoia. When the bark has been stripped, you have absolutely no protection when a fire comes raging into your life.

The biggest problem with denying God's sovereignty is that it goes directly against the clear teaching of Scripture. The Bible teaches that God alone is the holy, good, and absolute ruler over all.

He is sovereign.

He is *the* Sovereign.

And we aren't.

There was one ancient king who found himself up close and personal with this great truth. He is found in the book of Daniel, and his name is Nebuchadnezzar.

A SOVEREIGN TAKES NOTE OF *the* SOVEREIGN

King Nebuchadnezzar was king of Babylon during the time of the prophet Daniel. He was the most powerful man on the face of the earth. He was the absolute sovereign in his kingdom.

And it went to his head.

Nebuchadnezzar completely forgot about the sovereign God upon whom he depended every moment for breath. He became puffed up in his pride and began to believe his own press clippings. He should have known better, because He had already been exposed to the true Sovereign, the God of Israel. He'd had a very disturbing dream one night—a dream that was somehow more than a dream and shook him to the core. And he wanted to know what it meant. In most such situations, he would tell his advisors of the dream, and they would interpret it for him. But this dream was like no other he had ever experienced. And he didn't want spin; he wanted to know what it *meant*. So he declared that his advisors needed to first tell him what his dream was and then interpret it.

And if they didn't, he would start killing them off one by one.

When it was Daniel's turn to appear before the king, the prophet related the king's dream and its interpretation in precise and stunning detail. Such a revelation could have only come from God Himself! In that moment, Nebuchadnezzar knew that Daniel's God, the God of Israel, was the one true God. The evidence set before Him was undeniable.

But he soon forgot about Him. In fact, he built a golden idol and commanded everyone to bow before it. Daniel's three friends were brought to the king because they refused to bow. In a fit of rage, the king had these three courageous young Israelis thrown into a furnace so hot that it killed the men who threw them in. Yet these three young Jews walked around in the flames without a hair on their head being singed. As Nebuchadnezzar watched this unfold, his disbelieving eyes saw that there were *four* men in the furnace— although only three had gone in. The fourth was the Son of God Himself.

Nebuchadnezzar had witnessed for himself the power of the one true God. Deep down, he knew very well that there was a God in heaven who was the King of kings. A short time after this miraculous expression of God's power, the king had a recurring dream. None of his advisors could interpret it for him. But Daniel, through the power of God, interpreted the dream and told Nebuchadnezzar exactly what was going to happen in the future. And it wasn't a pretty picture.

Because Nebuchadnezzar had refused in his heart to bow before God, God was going to give him the mind of a beast and send him out to graze with the cattle for seven years. Instead of bowing right then before God and pleading for mercy, however, Nebuchadnezzar hardened his heart once again and ignored the warning of Daniel. One year later, as the king was walking on his rooftop, admiring all he had built (the hanging gardens of Babylon were one of the seven wonders of the world), and congratulating himself for his brilliance, something suddenly snapped in Nebuchadnezzar's mind. Even as he was giving himself a virtual Oscar for personal greatness and power, here is what happened:

"The king reflected and said, 'Is this not Babylon the great, which I myself have built as a royal residence by the might of my power and for the glory of my majesty?' While the word was in the king's mouth, a voice came from heaven, saying, 'King Nebuchadnezzar, to you it is declared: sovereignty has been removed from you, and you will be driven away from mankind, and your dwelling place will be with the beasts of the field. You will be given grass to eat like cattle, and seven periods of time will pass over you until you recognize that the Most High is ruler over the realm of mankind and bestows it on whomever He wishes.' Immediately the word concerning Nebuchadnezzar was fulfilled; and he was driven away from mankind and began eating grass like cattle, and his body was drenched with the dew of heaven until his hair had grown like eagles' feathers and his nails like birds' claws." (Daniel 4:30–33)

This particular illness has since been documented by psychologists as a rare form of monomania. This rare disorder, called boanthropy, is one in which a person imagines himself to be a cow or bull and acts accordingly. Untreated patients have been known to wander in fields, eat certain grasses, and drink from puddles and ponds. The fundamental physical abnormality is that of long hair and coarse, thickened fingernails.[62]

For the next seven years, the greatest king on earth grazed with the cattle in the field because he refused to acknowledge the sovereignty of God.

"But at the end of that period, I, Nebuchadnezzar, raised my eyes toward heaven and my reason returned to me, and I blessed the Most High and praised and honored Him who lives forever; for His dominion is an everlasting dominion, and His kingdom endures from generation to generation. All the inhabitants of the earth are accounted as nothing, but He does according to His will in the host of heaven and among the inhabitants of earth; and no one can ward

off His hand or say to Him, 'What have You done?'"
(Daniel 4:34–35)

Nebuchadnezzar let us in on the secret that he learned firsthand: "God's dominion is total: He wills as He chooses and carries out all that He wills, and none can stay His hand or thwart His plans."[63]

DANGER AHEAD

We have arrived at a very dangerous point in this chapter. I use the word *dangerous* for a reason. The danger is that you will stop reading, because what we are about to jump into is going to require you to think. I mean *really* think.

It will not entertain you.

But it just may save your life.

Some great man in the past observed that "we are entertaining ourselves to death." But how do you survive when your five-year-old daughter is diagnosed with leukemia? What do you do when your wife leaves you for some guy she met over the Internet or your husband goes after a trophy wife at midlife? What do you do when you were laid off a year ago and you still can't find work?

Entertainment won't cut it when your life is falling apart.

But the sovereignty of God will hold you together and keep you from losing your mind. The sovereignty of God is your two feet of bark. And when the fires come raging over the next ridge (and they will), you won't last long without it.

For that reason, let me urge you to hang on as we dive a little deeper into Scripture.

The Bible tells us that God owns it all, He rules over it all, and He ordains it all.

God Owns It All

Do you remember the three lies in chapter one? The first lie is that you can have it all. On the contrary, God already owns it all. Because He is a good and gracious God, He gives us good gifts throughout our lives. But make no mistake—we may possess some of it for a time, but He is sovereign and He owns it all.

> "Whatever is under the whole heaven is Mine."
> (Job 41:11)

> The earth is the LORD'S, and all it contains, the world, and those who dwell in it. (Psalm 24:1)

Did you take a hit when the stock market fell apart? If so, you may be wondering how you will put your kids through college, or how you will survive when you retire. Have you lost your job? If so, you're probably wondering how you will make your mortgage payment this month.

God knows how much your mortgage is, and He knows how much it will take to get your kids through college. He knows what you need and *when* you need it. And He will give it to you at the right time. "No good thing does He withhold from those who walk uprightly" (Psalm 84:11).

God Rules Over All

God rules over everything. He rules over Saddam Hussein, North Korea, al-Qaida, and anything or anyone else you can think of.

> The LORD has established His throne in the heavens, and His sovereignty rules over *all*. (Psalm 103:19)

> *"All* authority has been given to Me in heaven and on earth," [said Jesus], the blessed and only Sovereign, the King of kings and Lord of lords. (Matthew 28:18; 1 Timothy 6:15)

The "all" of these verses refers to every power in the heavens and on the earth. God raises up rulers and puts them down.

> Behold, the nations are like a drop from a bucket, and are regarded as a speck of dust on the scales.... It is He who sits above the circle of the earth, and its

inhabitants are like grasshoppers, who stretches out the heavens like a curtain and spreads them out like a tent to dwell in. He it is who reduces rulers to nothing, who makes the judges of the earth meaningless. Scarcely have they been planted, scarcely have they been sown, scarcely has their stock taken root in the earth, but He merely blows on them, and they wither, and the storm carries them away like stubble.... "I, the LORD, am the first, and with the last. I am He." (Isaiah 40:15, 22–24; 41:4)

Does the "all" of these verses include Satan and his angels? It *especially* includes Satan and all who serve him. Although Satan is the ruler of darkness and the slave master of this world, his power is limited. Even Satan cannot help but promote the purposes of God. "The LORD has made everything for its own purpose, even the wicked for the day of evil" (Proverbs 16:4).

B. B. Warfield once said, "The devil thinks that he is free, but he has the bit in his mouth, and God holds the reins."

God Has Ordained It All

Ordain means "to establish or order by appointment or decree."

The Bible says that God has ordained the end from the

beginning. God has ordained all things, and nothing occurs apart from His plan and consent.

> "For the LORD of hosts has planned, and who can frustrate it? And as for His stretched-out hand, who can turn it back?" (Isaiah 14:27)

> [God] works all things after the counsel of His will. (Ephesians 1:11)

> The counsel of the LORD stands forever, the plans of His heart from generation to generation. (Psalm 33:11)

> "My purpose will be established, and I will accomplish all My good pleasure." (Isaiah 46:10)

> God's not only *knows* your future; He has *ordained* it.

> Many plans are in a man's heart, but the counsel of the LORD will stand. (Proverbs 19:21)

> Not a leaf or a sparrow falls without the permission of God.

> Are not two sparrows sold for a penny? Yet not one of

them will fall to the ground apart from the will of your Father. (Matthew 10:29, NIV)

God knows every hair on your head. He knows every beat of your heart. He knew who your mother and father would be, and if He chooses to give you children He knows who they will be...and their children...and their children. Before time began He knew the date of your birth. And He knows the day you will die. He knows all this *because He has ordained it.*

Your eyes have seen my unformed substance; and in Your book were all written the days that were ordained for me, when as yet there was not one of them. (Psalm 139:16)

God knows what you are thinking and the decisions you will make. And even as you are making them, He is accomplishing His plan. As Solomon wrote, "The mind of man plans his way, but the LORD directs his steps" (Proverbs 16:9).

MOLECULAR THEOLOGY

R. C. Sproul summed it up when he said, "in God's universe, there is not one maverick molecule."

"He is before all things, and in Him *all things hold together"* (Colossians 1:17).

God has absolute control over worlds and planets, over black holes and asteroids hurtling through space, over atoms and atomic bombs, over godless murderers and godly believers—over every moment in time and history. And, praise be, over its ultimate conclusion.

This means that in *your* world there is not one maverick molecule. There are no "accidents" or senseless events. And there are no blessings that have not ultimately come from His hand.

God is in complete control, and you are not. God is in charge, and you are not. God knows the future, and you do not. God determines the blessings as well as the difficulties you will encounter in this life, and you cannot.

God is sovereign in your marriage. He is sovereign in the lives of each one of your children. His is sovereign over your job. He is sovereign over your boss. He is sovereign over the corporation that is about to buy out the corporation that you work for. He is sovereign over your health. He is sovereign over your 401(k) and your stock market portfolio (if you still have one). He is sovereign over the swirl of world affairs that greets you in the news every day. He is sovereign over the flight you just missed...or caught.

He is sovereign over your decisions, *even when they are bad ones.*

This is unfathomable. It is too high. It is too big for us to grasp.

Yet when you begin to live in the light of God's sovereign nature, something happens. Suddenly you are able to see life from a different perspective.

If God is sovereign, why drive yourself into the ground going 24/7?

If God is sovereign, why should you stay up all night and worry?

If God is sovereign, then everything is *not* on your shoulders. Everything is on *His* shoulders.

THE SOVEREIGN WEIGHT LIFTER

As you may have guessed, C. H. Spurgeon had a grip on the sovereignty of God. And for this reason, this particular doctrine literally flowed through his teaching. Once he was teaching on Matthew 11:28–30, when he painted a poignant word picture of God:

> Oh! It is a happy way of smoothing sorrow, when we can say, "We will wait only upon God." Oh ye agitated Christians, do not dishonor your religion by always wearing a brow of care; come, cast your burden upon the Lord. I see ye staggering beneath a weight which He would not feel. What seems to you a crushing burden, would be to Him but as the

small dust of the balance. See! The Almighty bends His shoulders, and He says, "Here, put thy troubles here."[64]

God is the great weight lifter. The burden that weighs us clear down to the ground is but dust upon His great shoulders. He leans down with His powerful shoulders and says, "Come to Me, all who are weary and heavy-laden, and I will give you rest" (Matthew 11:28).

Have you given your life to Jesus? Is He your Sovereign?

Then it's time for you to lay down your burden, lean back upon His strong arms, and rest.

LINGERING QUESTIONS

Perhaps you believe in God's sovereignty. Perhaps you are convinced that His sovereign nature is biblical and true. So the lingering question in your mind is not about His sovereignty. The lingering question for you has to do with His trust-worthiness. You may be saying, "Yes, God is the King, but is He a King who can be trusted?" For many believers, this is the crux of their struggle. What if I am not happy with His ordained plan? And how do my own choices come into the picture?

These are valid, important questions.

And for this reason we will spend the next chapter looking at God's answer. We will discover how human responsibility fits into the picture. And we will look closely at the character of our King.

But before we move forward, I want to show you just one example of the tenderness and kindness of God.

Just before September 11, Todd and Lisa had a wonderful week together in Rome. Todd had won a sales contest, and the trip to Rome was the award. Little did they know how special that trip would be. During the week in Rome, Lisa grabbed a few minutes here and there to prepare for the women's Bible study that would start the following week at her home church.

Interestingly enough, the passage in her study guide for the first week's lesson was Romans 11:33–36, the verses that had been so meaningful to her about the sovereignty of God.

They returned home to New Jersey on September 10, and the rest is history. But several months later, after the FBI finished its investigation, Lisa discovered something that she would cherish forever.

In a search for evidence, the FBI impounded all the cars belonging to passengers aboard Flight 93. After officials released the car, Lisa had friends remove all of Todd's belongings and store them for her to look through later.

"One item they found," Lisa says, "was intriguing."

In the armrest tray between the front bucket seats, Todd had some Scripture memorization cards that he used while driving. The top card on the stack, the one that he would have read on his way to the airport on the morning of September 11, was Romans 11:33–36, (NIV):

"Oh, the depth of the riches of the wisdom and knowledge of God! How unsearchable his judgments, and his paths beyond tracing out! 'Who has known the mind of the Lord? Or who has been his counselor? Who has ever given to God, that God should repay him?' For from him and through him and to him are all things. To him be the glory forever! Amen."

It was the exact passage of Scripture that had helped me through my questions following my dad's death; the same passage I'd been reminded of at Wheaton College; and the very passage that had been my memory verses for the Bible study I was preparing in Rome, the week before Todd died.[65]

How kind is our great Sovereign! The verse that had been in Lisa's heart over the years was the verse that Todd was putting in his heart. They both believed in the sovereignty of God. They were both counting on the sovereignty of God. And the knowledge that her husband had put that specific verse in his heart before he boarded United Flight 93 was a special assurance to Lisa that God does all things well. Even when it runs contrary to what we think is best.

Todd stepped into that plane with Romans 11:33–36 tucked in his heart.

Knowing that did something for Lisa.

Quite frankly, it lightened her load.

Two feet of bark will do that for you.

Chapter Eight

Two Slabs of Timber:
You Need a Savior

*"Knowing that I am not the one in control
gives great encouragement.
Knowing the One who is in control is everything."*

Alexander Michael

*"Some providences of God, like Hebrew letters, are
best understood backwards."*

Thomas Watson

Sherlock Holmes and Dr. Watson went on a camping trip. They pitched their tent under the stars and then went to sleep. In the middle of the night, Holmes awakened and exclaimed, "Watson, look up and tell me what you deduce."

Watson opened his eyes, and said, "I see billions and billions of stars. It's likely that some of these stars have planetary systems. Furthermore, I deduce that there is probably oxygen on some of these planets, and it's possible that life has developed on a few of them. Is that what you observe?"

Holmes replied, "No, you idiot. Somebody stole our tent!"

It's possible to miss the obvious when it comes to the sovereignty of God. The obvious reality is that a king is only as good as his character. Therein lies our hope. Therein lies our rest.

The character of God lies at the very heart of His sovereign rule. God is not only the absolute ruler over all; He is the perfect and good ruler. And because He is, you can trust Him with your whole heart.

A person who trusts God with his whole heart doesn't carry the world on his shoulders.

A person who trusts God with his whole heart can survive whatever tough things come his way.

A person who trusts God with his whole heart will not be driven by fear and anxiety.

A person who trusts God with his whole heart can sleep at night.

Let me ask you a question.

Think of several people that you really trust. Why do

you trust them? Do you trust them because they have commanded you to trust them? Do you trust them because they have a lot of money or power? Do you trust them because of their achievements in life? If so, then your trust is misplaced. Most of us do not put our trust in someone for these reasons.

Most of us put our trust in those who have

- proven to be trustworthy,
- demonstrated their love for us,
- shown that they keep their word and their commitments,
- proven themselves to be people of honor and integrity.

A man whose wife trusts him has consistently chosen to be faithful to her in very tangible ways. He refuses to look at other women. He rejects the pull of pornography and turns off the TV when it flaunts sexual promiscuity. He expresses his love to her by serving her. He stays committed when the tough times come. He tries hard to communicate consistently and resolve conflicts with his wife.

Likewise, a man who trusts his wife does so because of the love she has demonstrated toward him, over and over. He trusts her because he knows that she is on his team, she believes in him, and she seeks to meet his needs.

Trust is a valuable commodity that cannot be legislated. We tend to trust those who are trustworthy.

A TRUSTWORTHY SOVEREIGN

I recall the story of a poor woman in Scotland who was accused of stealing. She was brought to the sovereign leader of the clan. He ordered that she be taken to the beach, and that her long hair be tied to the rocks. Eventually the tide covered her face and did not recede until she was dead. She died a slow, horrible death because her sovereign had a horrible character.

Back in the days of kings, the importance of character was understood. If you happened to get a bad king, you were a miserable man. If you happened to get a good one, you were a fortunate man indeed.

By the way, let it never be said that America had no king. When our country was founded, our king was the Lord. And our democracy was a vehicle by which His laws could be established. A wealth of writing documents this fact. But only consider this one statement, issued by Samuel Adams on August 2, 1776, at the signing of the Declaration of Independence:

We have this day restored the Sovereign to Whom all men ought to be obedient. He reigns in heaven and from the rising to the setting of the sun, let His kingdom come.[66]

Today, American culture bows before another king. He comes disguised and wrapped up in the culture of self, but he is nonetheless the deceiver, the evil one. Mark it down; democracy without the sovereign King will eventually succumb to chaos and tyranny. It has been said that democracy is only as good as the people in it. But to take it a step further, those people are only as good as the king they choose to serve in their hearts. We all "gotta serve somebody," as Bob Dylan used to sing.

What kind of character does the sovereign King of the universe possess? This is the bottom line. If God is less than wholly trustworthy, it doesn't matter that He is sovereign, and we Christians are to be most pitied.

But if He is a trustworthy Sovereign, then we would be foolish not to put our faith in Him.

THE AUTOBIOGRAPHY OF GOD

I enjoy a good biography.

David McCullough's recent biography of John Adams is one of the best I've read in years. No one expected it to become a runaway bestseller, but it took off like gangbusters. People who had never in their lives read a serious biography were going out and buying it. What was the uncanny appeal of this book? There is no question that McCullough's writing was masterful, and certainly the integrity and common sense of this great man was a breath of fresh air against the backdrop of present-day politics.

But I think this book's greatest appeal lies in the fact that it is largely an autobiography by the dead man himself. John Adams and his wife, Abigail, left behind voluminous notes, journals, and diaries. John began keeping a daily account of his thoughts at the age of fifteen. And both he and his wife kept copies of every letter they ever wrote. Since they had to be apart for much of their marriage—and there were no telephones—the letters between this couple flowed back and forth for nearly a half century.

John and Abigail were genuine partners and lovers throughout their lives. And since they were both expressive and opinionated, they had no difficulty in putting their thoughts down in writing to one another. As a result, these letters are a treasure trove of their innermost thoughts and feelings, and of otherwise unknown "inside details" of the people and events of their day. They have preserved a most riveting story that no biographer could have conceived.

The Bible is essentially God's autobiography. "In the beginning God…" (Genesis 1:1).

It is God's revelation to us about Himself. It is His unfolding to us of His plan for the ages.

Paul tells us in Romans 1 that everyone knows of God. We know of Him through nature. And we know of Him because the truth of His existence has been written on our hearts. Hebrews 1 goes on to say that we know of Him because He has chosen to reveal Himself through "the prophets in many portions and in many ways," and finally, because He "has spoken to us in His Son." Jesus is "the *exact representation of His nature,* and upholds all things by the word of His power" (Hebrews 1:1–3). John tells us, "The Word became flesh, and dwelt among us, and *we saw His glory,* glory as of the only begotten from the Father, *full of grace and truth*" (John 1:14).

We never have to wonder about the character of God. For it has been revealed and demonstrated to us. But two aspects of God's character are especially important when it comes to his sovereignty. One is often discussed among believers. The other is rarely mentioned.

Let's begin with the attribute that is often discussed, yet so easily forgotten.

God Is Good

Mary tells the following story:

> Some time ago I was going through a time of deep sadness. The grief would come upon me at unsuspecting moments, while driving in the car, standing in a grocery store line, or just working around the house. My youngest son, who was then eighteen, tuned into my grief and could sense it even when I thought I was hiding it well. One day he came in and

hugged me. Then he looked at me and said, "Mom, God is good. You cannot forget that He is truly good." He was right, and at that time in my life I needed to be reminded of this great truth.

Our King is a good King.

Do you remember the little prayer that children used to say before meals? "God is great; God is good. Let us thank Him for our food." Perhaps we should reinstitute this prayer. For God is entirely and altogether good.

We are all recipients of God's goodness. By His goodness, the rain falls on the just and the unjust. But for those who love the Lord, God is uniquely good.

O taste and see that the LORD is good; how blessed is the man who takes refuge in Him! (Psalm 34:8)

How great is Your goodness, which You have stored up for those who fear You. (Psalm 31:19)

We have a friend who has fully embraced the goodness of God. Whenever you ask her how she is doing, she always begins by saying, "God is good." It is her trademark. Lisa grew up in a tough situation. Her mother was an alcoholic, and her father abandoned the family, moving from one wife to another. In her growing-up years she had to make her own way, taking care of herself and surviving on very little. But the turning point of her life came in high school when she encountered Jesus Christ. When she gave her life to Him, He changed her forever. Lisa then embraced the goodness of God. Life has not been a bed of roses since then, but God has honored her faith and abundantly blessed her. That's why we like to be around her. Because no matter what her circumstances, she is always reminding us of God's goodness.

Our God has more goodness than any man or woman who has ever lived. Than *all* the men and women who have ever lived, put together! The very best men and women cannot begin to equal the goodness of God. This is because God's goodness rises out of His holiness, His justice, and His love. Consider this with me for a moment:

God Is Holy

Holiness means purity.[67]
Is there something God cannot do? Yes. He cannot sin.

"Holy, Holy, Holy, is the Lord God, the Almighty,
who was and who is and who is to come."
Revelation 4:8)

God is utterly righteous and perfect in all that He does. Even the demons recognize his holiness. They cried out to

Jesus, "Ha! What do you want with us, Jesus of Nazareth? Have you come to destroy us? I know who you are—the Holy One of God!" (Luke 4:34, NIV).

When you consider God's goodness, remember that it rises out of his holiness.

God Is Just

God is eminently fair and just in all that He does.

The psalmist declared: "Righteousness and justice are the foundation of Your throne" (Psalm 89:14). Moses sang, "Ascribe greatness to our God! The Rock! His work is perfect, for all His ways are just; a God of faithfulness and without injustice, righteous and upright is He" (Deuteronomy 32:3–4).

Of late, there have been many disappointing decisions in our courts of law.

Judges have thrown out verdicts because of politics. State courts have ignored the law and made up their own. Laws have been changed or eradicated to adjust to our lowering morality. The Supreme Court of our land has refused to acknowledge the sanctity of unborn life.

But let us not forget. God alone is *the* Supreme Court. His laws are perfect and His judgments are true. The day is coming when every judge will stand before the Lord. The day is coming when God will judge the living and the dead, and all will be put right.

The justice of God is what led Jesus to the cross. "For Christ also died for sins once for all, the *just* for the *unjust*" (1 Peter 3:18). Jesus died in our place so that God's justice might be satisfied and mercy might be made available to all.

The Cross is the greatest act of justice in history.

But God also judges in this life. His justice comes in several forms. It comes in the sad and unavoidable consequences of sin in people's lives. These consequences come in various forms to all who disobey God's law—in ruined relationships, in inner futility, in empty and vain accomplishments, in pains brought on by a sinful lifestyle. And sometimes God's judgment comes in the form of bad rulers over a wayward people. The psalmist Asaph once struggled with what he perceived to be the ease and wealth of the wicked. Later, however, he came to realize God's justice.

> Surely in vain I have kept my heart pure…then I perceived their end. Surely You set them in slippery places; You cast them down to destruction. (Psalm 73:13, 17–18)

God has also promised a special justice for those who trust in Him and walk humbly before Him:

> They who seek the LORD shall not be in want of any good thing…. The eyes of the LORD are toward the

righteous and His ears are open to their cry…. The LORD is near to the brokenhearted and saves those who are crushed in spirit. (Psalm 34:10, 15, 18)

God also works on behalf of those who have been victimized by injustice:

O LORD, You have heard the desire of the humble; You will strengthen their heart, You will incline Your ear to vindicate the orphan and the oppressed. (Psalm 10:17–18)

When you consider God's goodness, remember that it rises out of His great passion for justice. Will you allow me to once again quote C. H. Spurgeon? Spurgeon said:

He who counts the stars and calls them by their names, is in no danger of forgetting His own children. He knows your case as thoroughly as if you were the only creature He ever made, or the only saint He ever loved.

God Is Love

Finally, God's goodness can be summed up in the word *love*. God loves every man, woman, and child. Jesus demonstrated that.

"For God so loved the world…" (John 3:16)

But God demonstrates His own love toward us, in that while we were yet sinners, Christ died for us. (Romans 5:8)

Jesus was a man of undisputed compassion and sacrificial love.

Seeing the people, He felt compassion for them, because they were distressed and dispirited like sheep without a shepherd. (Matthew 9:36)

"Greater love has no one than this, that one lay down his life for his friends." (John 15:13)

But God also has a special kind of love for those who follow after Him. In the Old Testament, this special love is summed up in the word *lovingkindness.* This word (the original Hebrew word is *hesed*) speaks of the God who is *always faithful, true to His promises, merciful, kind, gracious in all His dealings.*

But You, O Lord, are a God merciful and gracious, slow to anger and abundant in lovingkindness and truth. (Psalm 86:15)

"Hesed" flows through the pages of the Old Testament. The next time someone says to you that the God of the Old Testament is a vengeful God, take them to the passages which speak of God's lovingkindness. They will be exhausted before you have finished looking at hundreds of such passages. Our "slow to anger," merciful God is unlike any other god (lowercase) known to men.

In the New Testament, His essence can be summed up in the simple statement, "God *is* love" (1 John 4:8, 16). *The underlying motive for all that God does is love.* The word for love here (the original Greek word is *agape*) is a special kind of God-love.

First Corinthians 13 tells us about "agape." It is

- *spontaneous,* initiated by God;
- *selfless,* not caring about what it can gain, but what it can give;
- *active,* involving both *feelings* and the decisive *will to act* on our behalf;
- *unconditional,* not being contingent in any way upon the one loved.

You and I cannot fathom such a love. We cannot comprehend a love that is unaffected by our performance. We cannot grasp a love that never changes or wanes. My friend Stu Weber likes to say: "There is nothing you can ever do that can keep God from loving you."

Now that's something to live on!

There's something to take off the pressure.

God is holy. He is just. He is love. Never has there been such a good king on earth.

Are you still with me?

I hope you are, because we are about to look at an attribute of God that is rarely discussed. Yet it is supremely important.

God Is Mysterious

Our Sovereign is good. And He is also mysterious.

A great element of mystery surrounds God's attributes and character. John Piper has said it well:

> How God governs all events in the universe without sinning, and without removing responsibility from man, and with compassionate outcomes is mysterious indeed![68]

When I speak here of *mystery,* I am not thinking of Sherlock Holmes. Nor am I using it as the modern scientist would. The "mysteries" on Nova are *attainable* mysteries. They are mysteries only in that they are yet to be unraveled by man. Given the right intelligence, education, and time, someone will untie their knots, providing God allows it.

No, the mystery of God is another kind of mystery. We will *never* unravel it, no matter how much information we may gather. We will *never* comprehend or define it in our finite, sinful state.

"Trust in the LORD with all your heart and do not lean on your own understanding," says the writer of Proverbs (3:5). One reason we should not—dare not—lean on our own understanding is because we will never fully comprehend our God.

Our God is a mysterious God. By His divine prerogative and wisdom, He has chosen to keep certain things secret. Perhaps He keeps them secret because they are beyond our understanding. Certainly He keeps them secret out of His great wisdom in His dealings with men. But whatever the case, He has chosen wisely and lovingly what to explain and what to leave unknown. His thoughts are not our thoughts. They are higher. They are infinitely wiser.

> "The secret things belong to the LORD our God, but the things revealed belong to us and to our sons forever, that we may observe all the words of this law." (Deuteronomy 29:29)

Who has directed the Spirit of the LORD, or as His counselor has informed Him? With whom did He consult and who gave Him understanding? And who taught Him in the path of justice and taught Him knowledge and informed Him of the way of under-standing? (Isaiah 40:13–14)

"For as the heavens are higher than the earth, so are My ways higher than your ways and My thoughts than your thoughts." (Isaiah 55:9)

Perhaps no one has ever come as close to capturing the sense of the mystery of God as William Cowper did in the hymn "God Moves in a Mysterious Way":

God moves in a mysterious way
His wonders to perform;
He plants his footsteps in the sea
And rides upon the storm.
Ye fearful saints, fresh courage take;
The clouds ye so much dread
Are big with mercy and shall break
In blessings on your head.
Judge not the Lord by feeble sense,
But trust him for his grace;
Behind a frowning providence
He hides a smiling face.
His purposes will ripen fast,
Unfolding every hour;

The bud may have a bitter taste,
But sweet will be the flower.

The philosopher who seeks to reason through and clearly understand the great mysteries of God will inevitably come up short. They will never be solved by the human mind on this side of heaven.

What then can we say regarding his mysterious workings?

Although we will never completely understand many of the mysteries of God, such as both the divine and human nature of Jesus or the inspiration of Scripture, there are two mysteries surrounding God's sovereignty that directly concern us here.

THE MYSTERY OF HUMAN RESPONSIBILITY

I will never forget the day one of my favorite seminary profs explained this biblical concept. Dr. Cook drew a large circle that covered the entire chalkboard. Then, within that huge circle he placed a tiny dot. The large circle, he said, is God's sovereign preordained will. The tiny dot is man's will. Man's decisions and choices are *inside of* God's will. Some theologians have tried to place man's will outside of God's will, but as soon as they do so they deny God's sovereignty and nullify the clear teaching of Scripture. This means that the mysterious plan of God contains *certainty without compulsion*.

God deemed it wise to bring human choice into the picture. We are not divine puppets or mannequins. Within this mystery lies the fact that God never causes evil. He never forces a man to do the right or wrong thing. "Let no one say when he is tempted, 'I am being tempted by God'; for God cannot be tempted by evil, and He Himself does not tempt anyone." (James 1:13)

Thomas Watson laid out this apparent contradiction with great precision:

> The wisdom of God is seen in this, that the sins of men shall carry on God's work; yet that He should have no hand in their sin. The Lord permits sin, but does not approve of it. He has a hand in the action in which sin is, but not in the sin of the action."[69]

When we look out from our little dot of human will, we must realize that God works His sovereign plan *through* our choices and decisions.

The mystery of human responsibility does not lessen the truth of it. And it is no excuse for passivity. Choices have consequences. Adam sinned, and the whole world was plunged into spiritual darkness. The daily choices you and I make largely determine what our lives will become. This is why we are urged to:

- Seek first the kingdom of God, for "all these things will be added to you" (Matthew 6:33).
- Fear the Lord, for "the fear of the LORD is the beginning of wisdom" (Proverbs 9:10).
- Build our houses on the rock of his Word, for then they will withstand the "floods" and the "winds" (Matthew 7:25).
- Search the Scriptures, for "in them [is] life" (John 5:39).
- Pray, for we "do not have because [we] do not ask" (James 4:2).
- Guard our hearts from sin and the evil one, for "from it flow the springs of life" (Proverbs 4:23).
- Flee from evil, for "when lust has conceived, it gives birth to sin; and when sin is accomplished, it brings forth death" (James 1:15).
- Seek the fellowship of other believers, for in so doing we "stimulate one another to love and good deeds" (Hebrews 10:24).

I could go on and on. The essence of the Christian life can be summed up in these words of human responsibility: Trust and obey.

Yet God is ever at work, mysteriously but surely, even in the choices of men. Watson says:

The fact of free agency confronts us with mystery, inasmuch as God's control over our free, self-determined activities is as complete as it is over anything else, and how this can be we do not know.[70]

When Christians embrace this mystery, it both motivates and encourages us. God uses our choices to direct us—our wise choices to bless us, our unwise choices to teach us. Even when His people sin, God is sovereignly at work, bringing about His good purposes. "You meant evil against me," said Joseph to his brothers, "but God meant it for good" (Genesis 50:20).

This is commonly known as providence. J. I. Packer says:

The doctrine of providence teaches Christians that they are never in the grip of blind forces (fortune, chance, luck, fate); all that happens to them is divinely planned, and each event comes as a new summons to trust, obey, and rejoice, knowing that all is for one's spiritual and eternal good (Romans 8:28).[71]

Why, then, do Christians suffer in many of the same ways as the rest of the world? Christians die in automobile accidents. Christians get cancer. Christians lose their businesses. In many parts of the world, Christians suffer and die for their faith. Life seldom looks like a cakewalk for believers.

Jesus made all this very clear when He said, "In the world you have tribulation" (John 16:33). And Peter said, "Do not be surprised at the fiery ordeal among you" (1 Peter 4:12).

The Bible says that when Jesus returns to earth, sin will be judged and brought to an end. He will wipe all our tears away, and death will be no more. But until that day, the wheat and the tares will grow in the same field, awaiting the great reaping of the harvest at the end of time. And pain and death will be the experience of all who live in this fallen world. Until our Lord's return, this will be the experience of every person... without exception.

I will tell you another thing I know to be true. If I never suffered, I would be of no value to Him in this world. I would be worthless. If God exempted me from all suffering, I would become self-sufficient and proud. How do I know this? Because I have seen this alarming propensity time and again in my life.

When I was a young pastor, I used to do a lot of counseling. Sometimes men would come into my office and tell me that they were depressed. *Depressed?* I would be thinking to myself. *What this guy needs to do is suck it up and move on!* Now I didn't say this, but I thought it. And I have no doubt that my lack of compassion came through in my counseling.

Then about five years into pastoring, I hit a wall. I found myself between churches, and for a solid year I had no job. I ended up driving a truck to put bread on the table. During this time, Mary became very sick. And many of my friends kept their distance. My sense of self-worth plummeted, and I felt that my life of ministry was over. About six months into this period of my life, I became deeply depressed. So depressed that I literally cried for several hours every day. That's when I really thought my life was over.

Then a friend who was a Christian counselor explained that my depression was much like what a Vietnam vet would experience after returning from war. It was entirely understandable. The body can only take so much stress, he said, before it breaks down. He also explained that, in time, I would recover—although I had trouble believing him. Out of necessity I eventually took a tiny church that was landlocked and had no potential for growth. Every Sunday morning I would cry all the way to church. I would get up and preach. And then I would cry all the way home. During this period I lived and preached in the Psalms.

It took a good two years to work my way out of this depression, and to see the blessing that God would bring from such a difficult time. But I must tell you this. When someone comes to me now and says, "I'm struggling with depression," they get my full attention.

God enables us to go through suffering for a purpose.

This is the hope for the believer. Sometimes He wants to teach us about ourselves. Sometimes He wants to build deep character and faith into our lives. Sometimes He wants to move us on to a new place. Sometimes He wants to show us His goodness in the heat of the fires. God always has something specific that He is doing in our lives through the hardship.

"We are mistaken," writes C. S. Lewis, "if we consider this world as some sort of grand hotel where our purpose is to find unending pleasure. We should never think that pain is unusual or extraordinary. Instead, we should see this world as a training ground for eternity."[72]

TWO SLABS OF TIMBER

That's exactly how Al Braca viewed the Christian life. Al was a corporate bond trader for Cantor Fitzgerald on the 105th floor of the Word Trade Center. Al was a committed Christian. But he hated his job. According to his wife, Jeannie, "he couldn't stand the environment. It was a world so completely out of touch with his Christian values. But he wouldn't quit. He was convinced that God wanted him to stay there, to be a light in the darkness. To that end, Al would freely share his faith with his coworkers, many of whom sarcastically nicknamed him "The Rev."

"They mocked him," Jeannie recalls, "but when horrible things happened in their lives, they always asked Al for prayer."[73]

Al was at his desk bright and early on September 11. Or to put it another way, he was at his post. After the plane slammed into the building several floors below, it soon became apparent that Al and his coworkers had no escape. Al's body was found in the rubble a week later.

But something unique happened as the flames and heat were making their way into Al's suite of offices that day:

Reports trickled in from friends and acquaintances. Some people on the 105th floor had made a last call or sent a final e-mail to a loved one saying that "a man" was leading people in prayer. A few referred to Al by name. The Bracas learned that Al had indeed been ministering to people during the attack. When he realized that they were trapped in the building and would not be able to escape, Al shared the gospel with a group of 50 co-workers and led them in prayer.[74]

John Newton once observed:

God often takes a course for accomplishing His purposes directly contrary to what our narrow views would prescribe. He brings a death upon our feelings, wishes, and prospects when He is about to give us the desire of our hearts.

It was the desire of Al and Jeannie Braca that Al would be able to lead a number of coworkers to Christ. They had been praying for that for years. And that's why Al couldn't bring himself to leave. He was burdened that God would use him to bring those people to Christ. That was his desire. But never in his wildest dreams could he have imagined how God would bring the answer.

Al is a vivid example of a man whose life was wrapped in two feet of bark. How did he come to such a place of security? Because he had met the One who was nailed to two slabs of timber. Jesus was the reason for his deep-seated security. And so Al led his friends to the cross in their darkest hour.

All of us will suffer in this life. Yet every trial is sifted through the hands of God. All of us will die. Yet even the time and means of our death have been determined by our Lord. And He has promised to carry us through to the other side.

Have you given your life to Jesus, the sovereign King who died for you on two slabs of timber? This is the place where you must begin if you wish to live under His good and gracious rule.

There is one other mystery that comes up often, in light of God's sovereignty.

THE MYSTERY OF EVIL

Many have asked the question, "Why did God ordain a plan that included both the possibility of evil and the inevitability of its occurring?" The answer is that it is a mystery. Throughout history, men have tried to unravel it. But it will never be done.

G. K. Chesterton once observed the insanity of trying to figure out the unfathomable. "The poet only asks to get his head into the heavens. It is the logician who seeks to get the heavens into his head. And it is his head that splits."[75]

God's ways are not our ways and His thoughts are not our thoughts (see Isaiah 55:8). You have a much better chance of getting a Boeing 747 into your two-car garage than you do of understanding this mystery. It's not going to happen—not on this earth, anyway.

Volumes have been written on the question of evil. But when we get right down to it, God has not chosen to explain it. He did not explain it to Job, He hasn't explained it to Lisa Beamer or to Jeannie Braca, and He does not explain it to us. He has chosen, rather, to assert His holy character and purposes in all that He has ordained. And in this, Job, Lisa, and Jeannie eventually came to rest.

God has given us a tiny ray of insight into the heavens,

however. What has He revealed to us? He has provided *redemption* from evil through the costly death of His Son.

God's profound answer to us regarding the question of evil is *Jesus and the cross.* Two slabs of timber are God's answer to evil. The King became the Deliverer. The Sovereign became the Savior. In this we must rest.

All Things for Good

May I be frank? Satan wants us to stumble over him. It gives him supreme pleasure to plunder our faith.

The reality of living in a fallen and cursed world is that everyone suffers. Everyone has disappointments. Everyone dies. We must not blame God for this. We must, rather, thank God that every suffering in our lives is purposeful and that He has promised to give us everything we need in the midst of it.

One of my favorite Christian writers, as you may have guessed, is Thomas Watson. Watson was a great preacher in England in the 1600s. In 1662, this godly preacher, along with two thousand other preachers, was thrown out of the church in the Great Ejection. The Church of England—which was the *only* church in that era—took all of the "nonconformists," the Bible-teaching preachers, and in one fell swoop put them out of the churches. They lost their homes and their incomes, and they could never preach again. They were put in jail by the thousands.

That happened to Thomas Watson. He lost everything. But in 1663, he wrote a book called *All Things for Good*. He wrote it to encourage his fellow ministers who had also lost everything. The first chapter of the book is entitled "The Best Things Work for Good to the Godly." The second chapter is entitled "The Worst Things Work for Good to the Godly."

Watson believed God when He said that He causes all things to work together for *good* to those who love Him and are called according to His purpose (see Romans 8:28).

There was tremendous overload in Watson's life. But he overcame overload by holding on to the sovereignty of God. He believed the promise of God. He believed that God would turn his great loss into good.

You have a choice as to how you will handle the hard things in your life. You can become bitter and turn away from God. Or you can draw near to the Lord and reap the rich reward of his provision and care. You can insist that you are "entitled" to the happiness of your own choosing. Or you can trust God and give Him the room He needs to accomplish his gracious and wise plan in your life.

If God is your Father, if He knows what you need before you even ask, then He should be given the benefit of the doubt when life doesn't go according to your plan. You expect no less from your own children, who often don't know the big picture or understand what they truly need.

May I ask you a question?

What is the worst thing that has ever happened to you?

What is it that has put the deepest scar on your heart?

What is the wound in your life that has never quite healed because of your bitterness and resentment?

Can you trust His sovereignty and His promise in Romans 8:28?

Are you willing to live on this earth for the rest of your days with certain mysteries unsolved?

Are you willing to trust Him as David did in Psalm 27:13 when he wrote, "I would have despaired unless I had believed that I would see the goodness of the LORD."

There is no reason to despair.

The Sovereign is your Savior.

And His goodness is on the way.

That's the bark that will heal your wounds and the timber that will give you hope.

And in the process, it will lighten your load.

EPILOGUE
Dying to Live

Samuel Ward once observed, "to live well is to live twice."

This book has been an attempt from the Scriptures to discover how we can live well. But doing that is a process. And it's a process that involves life and death.

Madeline L'Engle, in looking back over her life, made a very insightful observation:

Our lives are a series of births and deaths; we die to one period and must be born to another. We die to childhood and are born to adolescence; to our high-school selves and (if we are fortunate) to our college selves; we die to our college selves and are born into the "real" world; to our unmarried selves and into our married. To become a parent is to birth a new self for the mother and father as well as for the baby.

When Hugh and I moved from the city to live year around at Crosswicks (the family farm), this was death to one way of life and birth to another. Then nine years later when we took our children, aged seven, ten, and twelve, out of a big house, a quiet village, a small country school, and moved back to New York and the world of the theatre, this was another experience of death and birth.[76]

Overcoming overload also involves a process. That process will entail a series of births and deaths. We must die to the addictive concept of 24/7. When we do, we can be born into the sweet savor of enjoying a Sabbath.

We must die to the triplet lies of *having* it all, *doing* it all, and *deserving* it all. Those are the lies of affluenza, and affluenza can be terribly destructive. Out of those deaths comes the joy of giving back to God the first of the good fruits He has given to us.

We die to the noise of the surrounding world by choosing to build a sanctuary to hear the voice of God. And in that sanctuary we die to the opinions of men and live abundantly from the truth of God's Word. So, too, we are learning to die to ourselves and live as we embrace the sovereignty of our good and gracious God.

None of this will happen overnight. We will experience some failures along with the victories. But we will stay with it. For we want to live well. And to live well is to live to the glory of God.

The publisher and author would love to hear your comments about this book. *Please contact us at:*
www.multnomah.net/farrar

NOTES

1. Richard Swenson, *Hurtling Toward Oblivion* (Colorado Springs, Colo.: NavPress, 1999), 31.
2. Ibid., 32.
3. Ibid.
4. Ibid., 34.
5. Roger Von Oech, *Expect the Unexpected or You Won't Find It* (San Francisco: Berrett-Koehler Publishers, 2002), 25.
6. J. I. Packer and Carolyn Nystrom, *Never Beyond Hope* (Downers Grove, Ill.: InterVarsity Press, 2000), 11.
7. John Piper, *Desiring God* (Sisters, Ore.: Multnomah Publishers, 1986), 23.
8. Von Oech, *Expect the Unexpected,* 130.
9. John Murray, *Principles of Conduct* (Grand Rapids, Mich.: Wm. B. Eerdmans Publishing Co., 1957), 42.
10. Ibid., 43–44.
11. Bruce A. Ray, *Celebrating the Sabbath: Find Rest in a Restless World* (Phillipsburg, N.J.: P&R Publishing, 2000), 46.

12. Ibid., 48.

13. James M. Stifler, *The Epistle to the Romans* (Chicago: Moody Press, 1960), 224.

14. Ray, *Celebrating the Sabbath,* 61.

15. David Ford, *The Shape of Living* (Grand Rapids, Mich.: Baker Books, 1997), 140.

16. Ibid., 134.

17. C. H. Spurgeon, *Lectures to My Students* (Grand Rapids, Mich.: Zondervan Publishers, 1954), 160.

18. Marva J. Dawn, *Keeping the Sabbath Wholly* (Grand Rapids, Mich.: Wm. B. Eerdmans Publishing Co., 1989), 29.

19. Lawrence Downs, "Hawaiians Find an Unlikely Eden in Las Vegas," *The New York Times*, 27 October 2002. http://www.nytimes.com/2002/10/27/national/27V EGA.html (accessed 9 January 2003).

20. David Wells, *No Place for Truth* (Grand Rapids, Mich.: Wm. B. Eerdmans Publishing Co., 1993), n.p.

21. Ibid.

22. Dallas Willard, *The Spirit of the Disciplines* (Dallas: Word Publishing, 1988), n.p.

23. Robert Menschel, *Markets, Mobs, and Mayhem* (Hoboken, N.J.: John Wiley & Sons, 2002), cover notes.

24. Donald S. Whitney, *Spiritual Disciplines for the Christian Life* (Colorado Springs: NavPress, 1991), 187.

25. Ibid.

26. Brook S. Mason, "An Empire, Yes, but More Serene Than Martha's," *New York Times*, 28 April 2002, Business section, p. 4.

27. Ibid.

28. Ibid.

29. Ibid.

30. *World Book Encyclopedia* (1959), 15:7307.

31. Eric Scholosser, *Fast Food Nation* (New York: Houghton Mifflin, 2001), 54.

32. Patrick Quillin, "Malnutrition among Cancer Patients," *HealthWorld Online*. http://www.healthy.net/asp/templates/article.asp?PageType=Article&ID=518 (accessed 13 January 2003).

33. N. Woychuk, *The British Josiah* (St. Louis, Mo.: SMF Press, 2001), 125.

34. John F. Walvoord and Roy B. Zuck, *The Bible Knowledge Commentary* (Wheaton, Ill.: SP Publications, 1985), 646.

35. Ibid., 647.

36. J. D. Douglas, *Who's Who in Christian History* (Wheaton, Ill.: Tyndale House Publishers, 1992), 735.

37. Ibid.

38. Woychuk, *The British Josiah,* 18.

39. Douglas, *Who's Who in Christian History,* 684.

40. Woychuk, *The British Josiah,* 22.

41. Ibid., 35.

42. Ibid, 4–5.

43. Ibid, 5.

44. Ibid.

45. Ibid., 130.

46. Peter Maas, *The Terrible Hours* (New York: Harper Collins Publishers, 2001), n.p.

47. C. H. Spurgeon, *The Soul-Winner* (Grand Rapids, Mich.: Wm. B. Eerdmans Publishing Co., 1963), 152–153.

48. "Influenza," in *Encyclopedia Britannica* (Chicago: Encyclopedia Britannica, Inc., 1964), 12:347.

49. Cited by Bruce Shelley, *The Gospel and the American Dream* (Portland, Ore.: Multnomah, 1989), 133.

50. Dr. Ralph E. Minear, *Kids Who Have Too Much* (Nashville: Thomas Nelson, 1989), 35.

51. Randy Alcorn, *The Treasure Principle* (Sisters, Ore.: Multnomah Publishers, 2001), 51.

52. Andy Dappen, *Shattering the Two-Income Myth* (Brier, Wa.: Brier Books, 1997), n.p. Dappen has some good thoughts on this subject, but we must take exception to his statement that is doesn't matter

which spouse stays home full-time. It does matter to people who take the Scriptures as authoritative for their lives. Biblically speaking, God has entrusted the man to be the primary provider and the wife to be the primary caregiver.

53. Alcorn, *The Treasure Principle,* 61.

54. Ibid., 60–61.

55. Lisa Beamer, quoted in *World,* 17August 2002, front cover.

56. Lisa Beamer, *Let's Roll* (Wheaton, Ill.: Tyndale House Publishers, 2002), 82.

57. Ibid., 83–84.

58. Holly Peters, "Evangelicals on the Decline," The Biola Connection, Fall 2002, 9.

59. Ibid., 10.

60. Ibid.

61. Ibid., 13.

62. Roland Kenneth Harrison, *Introduction to the Old Testament* (Grand Rapids, Mich.: Wm. B. Eerdmans Publishing Co., 1969), 1116.

63. J. I. Packer, *Concise Theology* (Wheaton, Ill.: Tyndale House Publishers, 1993), 33. "The assertion of God's absolute sovereignty in creation, providence and grace is basic to biblical belief…the vision of God on throne—that is ruling, recurs (1 Kings 22:19; Isaiah 6:1; Ezekiel 1:26; Daniel 7:9; Revelation 4:2…) and

we are constantly told in explicit terms that the Lord (Yahweh) reigns as king, exercising dominion over tiny and great things alike (Exodus 15:18; Psalm 47:83; 96:10; 97; 99:1–5; 146:10; Proverbs 16:33; 21:1; Isaiah 24:23; 52:7; Daniel 4:34–35; 5:21–28; 6:26; Matthew 10:29–31)."

64. C. H. Spurgeon, *Spurgeon's Gems* (New York: Fleming H. Revel, n.d.), 88.

65. Beamer, *Let's Roll,* n.p.

66. William J. Federer, *America's God and Country: Encyclopedia of Quotations* (Saint Louis, Mo.: Amerisearch, Inc., 1999), 201.

67. Packer, *Concise Theology,* 43.

68. John Piper, Why I Do Not Say, "God Did Not Cause the Calamity, but He Can Use It for Good," *Desiring God Ministries,* 17 September 2001. http://www.desiringgod.org/library/fresh_words/20 01/091701.html (accessed 13 January 2003).

69. Thomas Watson, cited by I. D. E. Thomas, *A Puritan Golden Treasury* (Carlisle, Pa.: Banner of Truth, 1977), 121.

70. Ibid., 33–34.

71. J. I. Packer, *Concise Theology,* 55–56.

72. Terry W. Glaspey, *Not a Tame Lion: The Spiritual Legacy of C. S. Lewis* (Elkton, Md.: Highland Books, 1996), 128.

73. Christin Ditchfield, "A Light in the Darkness," *Focus on the Family*, 2002. http://www.family.org/fofmag/sh/a0021985.cfm (accessed 14 January 2003).

74. Ibid.

75. G. K. Chesterton, *Orthodoxy* (New York: Image/Doubleday, 1908), 11.

76. Madeline L'Engle, *The Summer of the Great-Grandmother* (San Francisco: Harper SanFrancisco, 1974), 52.

GOD'S STRENGTH IN TODAY'S UNSTABLE TIMES

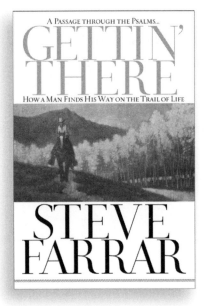

In *Gettin' There,* bestselling author Steve Farrar delves into the book of Psalms to give men a new sense of continuity, direction, purpose, and perspective. The Psalms are like a marked trail through life, showing that others have walked ahead and faced many of the challenges, temptations, heartaches, and perplexities that men will encounter on their journeys. Farrar shows that when a man begins to understand that the strong and caring hand of God is sovereign over everything in his life—including his trials and heartaches—his confidence, hope, and joy will increase dramatically in the God who created him and desires to use him. Now in paperback!

ISBN 1-57673-788-8

Men's conference speaker and bestselling author Steve Farrar takes readers through the Psalms to see how David endured crushing pressure and fiery trials and emerged a great man, shaped by the hand of God. Men facing difficult challenges in life will relate to chapters on Depression, Betrayal, When Your Family Is Falling Apart, Living with a Bad Decision, Living with Your Critics, and When Your Career Is Interrupted. Farrar encouragingly illustrates how David depended on God to overcome the same sins and trials—still remaining "a man after God's own heart."

ISBN 1-57673-892-2

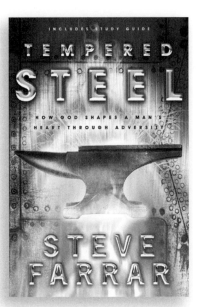

THE MEASURE OF A MAN

Instruction and motivation from bestselling author Steve Farrar

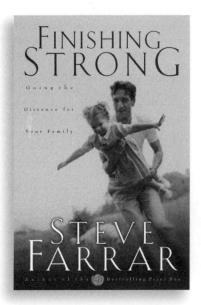

Every day, men see husbands and fathers around them falling to temptations such as workaholism, infidelity, uncontrolled anger, and ethical shortcuts. No man wants to hurt his wife and children. But if he is to "finish strong," living righteously and ethically to the end of his life, he must proactively implement the commitments he has made to Jesus Christ and to his family. In *Finishing Strong*, bestselling men's author Steve Farrar shows husbands and dads how they can do exactly that, teaching them how to recognize and avoid the pitfalls that can destroy a family and inspiring them to live with character and conviction.

ISBN 1-57673-726-8

"A leader must stand tall enough for his followers to find him. As the God-appointed captain of his family," says Steve Farrar, "a man faces the challenge of spying out the social territory, marking danger zones, and taking stands to protect those in his charge." It's an active leadership role—and Farrar's been training men to succeed in it for ten years. In this paperback rerelease of his popular *Standing Tall*, the men's ministries leader "walks tall" through America—observing politics, abortion, the gay movement, media trends, and the loss of our "moral boundaries." Farrar offers men sure biblical foundations on which to stand for faith-based living—closing with "Seven Ways to Help Your Kids Stand Tall." Study-guide appendix makes it great for group use, too!

ISBN 1-57673-788-8

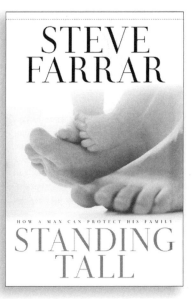

WAR HAS BEEN DECLARED ON THE AMERICAN FAMILY

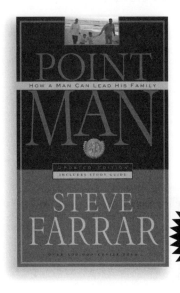

This bestselling classic encourages and equips Christian men to lead their families successfully through hazards and ambushes like divorce, promiscuity, suicide, and drug addiction. Men will find practical insight on topics such as a father's influence, maintaining purity, and husband-and-wife teamwork. In this war, renowned men's author Steve Farrar emphasizes, Jesus Christ is looking for men who will not die, but live for their families.

ISBN 1-59052-126-9

Over 240,000 Sold!

POINT MAN DEVOTIONAL

Since 1990, Steve Farrar's bestselling *Point Man* has helped thousands of men effectively guide their families through the moral chaos of today's society. Now, Farrar helps men dig deeper into God's Word for solid, biblical direction to help them meet this goal.

Building upon the crucial topics introduced in the book, *Point Man*, Farrar's devotional explores God's teachings about the subjects most important to husbands and fathers today. Each of these forty-five easy-to-complete readings includes: Scripture and devotional passages, key Bible verses, practical, personal applications, daily prayers, and more!

ISBN 0-88070-825-5

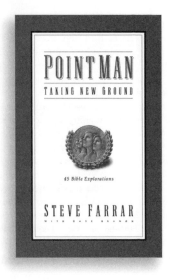

LONGING TO DISCOVER
LIFE'S BEST?

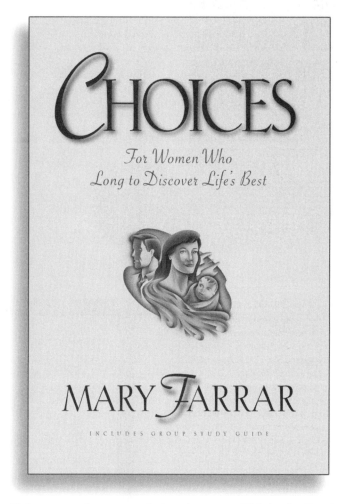

Today women have more choices than ever. This book of twelve lessons prepares women to make wise, God-aligned decisions in such vital areas as career, family, and personal growth. Each lesson has its own group study guide.

ISBN 0-88070-854-9